What people a

The Manifesto Handbook

I think a full-length book like this is long overdue, and it couldn't be better timed with the current climate of polarizing rhetoric, post-truth, Antifa, engaged art, etc. The brief history plus how-to lesson is a winning combination.
Mark Yakich, Distinguished Professor of English, Loyola University, New Orleans

A Wunderkammer of the aesthetics of revolution via revolutions in aesthetics, instructions included.
Joanna Walsh, author of *Break.up*

I am often suspicious of manifestos: they remind me of a more certain, mostly male-dominated, age, and I have grown impatient. But Julian Hanna's book, which might also be described as a love letter to the manifesto, has pierced my doubts, offering the manifesto as a tender literary object whose optimism still upholds the word as a dynamic, almost magical, device out of which whole worlds are created. His book has been an antidote to my cynicism.
Lucía Sanromán, Director of Visual Arts at Yerba Buena Center for the Arts, San Francisco

The Manifesto Handbook is something like a meta-manifesto, which proclaims the joy and necessity of the manifesto form. Julian Hanna shows us how to both read them and write them, to have some fun and maybe change the world. He also shows how this once distinctive form has soaked into the general style of writing of the internet age. But then the Manifesto has always found ways to outflank the received ideas and media habits of its era, no matter what the era. And in an era of cultural burnout and generalized depression, the short, sharp shot of mania that is the ground tone of the manifesto might not be a bad idea. Read this book, find your people, expose the enemy of the good life - and write your own!

McKenzie Wark, author of *A Hacker Manifesto*

Julian Hanna is an astute observer and critic of our world dominated by corporations and driven by technology. He is also a brilliant writer in his own right.

Andrew Gallix, Editor-in-Chief, 3:AM Magazine

Julian Hanna makes wisdom out of the most unreasonable of genres. A precious companion in a time of too much anger and not enough revolt.

Marta Peirano, author of *El Pequeño libro rojo del activista en la red* *(The Little Red Book of the Network Activist)*

The Manifesto Handbook

95 Theses on an Incendiary Form

The Manifesto Handbook

95 Theses on an Incendiary Form

Julian Hanna

Winchester, UK
Washington, USA

JOHN HUNT PUBLISHING

First published by Zero Books, 2019
Zero Books is an imprint of John Hunt Publishing Ltd., No. 3 East St., Alresford,
Hampshire SO24 9EE, UK
office@jhpbooks.com
www.johnhuntpublishing.com
www.zero-books.net

For distributor details and how to order please visit the 'Ordering' section on our website.

ISBN: 978 1 78535 898 2
978 1 78535 899 9 (ebook)
Library of Congress Control Number: 2018961987

A CIP catalogue record for this book is available from the British Library.

Design: Stuart Davies

UK: Printed and bound by CPI Group (UK) Ltd, Croydon, CR0 4YY
US: Printed and bound by Thomson-Shore, 7300 West Joy Road, Dexter, MI 48130

We operate a distinctive and ethical publishing philosophy in
all areas of our business, from our global network of authors to
production and worldwide distribution.

Contents

For Simone, Clyde & Nico

At a higher stage, everyone will become an artist, i.e., inseparably a producer-consumer of total culture creation...Everyone will be a Situationist, so to speak, with a multidimensional inflation of tendencies, experiences, or radically different "schools"—not successively, but simultaneously.

Situationist International, Situationist Manifesto (1960)

SCUM will keep on destroying, looting, fucking-up and killing until the money-work system no longer exists and automation is completely instituted...

Valerie Solanas, SCUM Manifesto (1967)

Preamble

I was born in Vancouver the same year as Greenpeace, just a few blocks away. My parents lived in a communal house on West Broadway. Then as now, the West Coast was a place of extreme contrasts. In the 1970s British Columbia was a hippie dream, a destination for idealistic young Americans (like the writer William Gibson) who had dodged the draft. In the 1980s Vancouver was the city of the future, constantly demolishing anything remotely old to make way for the new. Expo 86, with its SkyTrain and IMAX 3D theater, symbolized this future. In *City of Glass* (2000) Douglas Coupland called our hometown one of the world's youngest—which felt true when you walked around it. At the same time Canadians were finally starting to acknowledge the ancient history and land claim rights of the original inhabitants. Even my parents exhibited stark contrasts: my mother was quiet and gentle, a daycare worker who studied empathy, while my father went to work in the tense confines of a mental hospital (as they were called then). He was a nudist and prankster, more Yippie than hippie, a practical joker who swung between irreverent clowning and darker pronouncements.

They married on the day of the moon landing, my 19-year-old soon-to-be mother in a mini dress, then divorced when I was young like all of their friends. We moved from Vancouver to the Sunshine Coast and then to the island, where I drifted dreamily between their lives in the peaceful haze of a comfortable Canadian childhood. The public high school I attended had a distinctly colonial unreality about it: some of my fellow students spoke with English accents despite having never left Canada, and there were a group of mods who dressed in white and rode matching Vespas. There was a cricket club and something called the Existentialist Wine and Cheese Club, whose members wore eye patches and put on absurdist plays and read nihilist poetry while fencing with foils. It was a strange school set in the middle of nowhere, on an outcropping that dipped below the 49th parallel.

But there was also another world. My grandparents lived on the outskirts of town, across the highway from Western Speedway, an oval track with a rickety wooden grandstand in a clearing surrounded by tall pine trees. The Speedway held weekly stock car races, demolition derbies and monster truck shows. Every Sunday my mother and I used to visit the rust-red house on the hill, and the sound of those events—the announcer, the crowd, the collision of metal-on-metal—echoed through my childhood. "Big race at the Speedway tonight," my grandmother would say matter-of-factly, frying sausages in the Formica-topped kitchen as the radio played a mournful country and western song. Though it unnerved me as a kid, I was thrilled when my grandfather or my uncles would take me across the road to see a show. The best was hit-to-pass: huge, battered, hand-painted American stock cars sliding drunkenly around the blacktop, their engines a deafening roar, colliding with each other and sometimes bursting into flames as they tried to take the lead. It was a ritual as fascinating as it was brutal and pointless. I still get that *mémoire involontaire* when I smell burning rubber and gasoline.

The people who went to the Speedway were pretty rough. There was no existentialism or wine and cheese here. The men wore torn flannel shirts and mustaches and trucker hats, held cigarettes and plastic cups of beer; the women hollered; the whole place reeked of destruction. They sat in the wooden stands in the middle of a patch of industrial wasteland cleared from the forest that naturally covered everything and cheered at the spectacle of exploding cars. They struck me as different, because I was already steeping myself in the snobbish borrowed culture of the Old World. But these were my people. This was what I came from. Immigrant farmers on both sides who found themselves trapped in the frozen north of the Canadian prairies and headed west until they found somewhere livable. Western Speedway was my culture. I could read all the Sartre and Camus I wanted, but as I stood there in the stands flanked by my tall uncles, ex-servicemen who hunted elk and deer in the forest behind the rust-red house, I knew it was Paris and London that were strange and distant, not this place.

And yet I had the luxury of changing identities when I wanted to. I could dress in black and listen to cassettes of bands with avant-garde names like Cabaret Voltaire (after the home of Zurich Dada), Art of Noise (named for Luigi Russolo's 1913 Futurist manifesto: "Today, Noise triumphs and reigns supreme") and Magnetic Fields (after André Breton and Philippe Soupault's novel *Les champs magnetiques*, a founding Surrealist text). I could even return to the continent my ancestors fled or were expelled from, thinking they'd never return — I could work in a bookshop on the Left Bank or Charing Cross Road. But although I did eventually leave for good, I couldn't shake my love of the reckless and random New World: its untethered fluidity, its fresh starts and radical self-invention. Even more than the freedom I miss the booming and banging: destruction and rebirth, the theater of authenticity, nihilism as entertainment, consumerism as spectacle.

One particular event at the Speedway seems to sum it up best in hindsight: the sideshow in which adults and children pay money to smash up a brand new car with sledgehammers before it is sent out to race. The barely contained energy of the crowd, like some Marxist fever dream. The loudness and brashness of the New World. The hope mixed with *fuck you* of the frontier city. The endless heavy metal solo of everyday life. Years later I read of Marinetti's (not unproblematic) desire to "go out into the streets, lay siege to the theaters, and introduce the fist into the struggle for art." I loved it and all the extreme and desperate movements it spawned. Was the life I left behind and the place I tried to bury the very utopia those artists of the tired and crowded Old World dreamt of? Was this the freedom that Hannah Arendt found when she fled Nazi Germany (and Heidegger), through Madrid and Lisbon to the dynamism of New York? When I started reading manifestos, I found that they contained everything I'd ever wanted. They represented the perfect marriage of the real world and fantasy, the Western Speedway and the Cabaret Voltaire. Here lay the fire, the darkness, the excitement, the dreams, the blood and guts, the absurdity and humor, the hope and fear.

I have been thinking about manifestos on and off for 2 decades. I caught the obsession as a student in Montreal, capital of disreputable desires (in Canada at least). I needed a few extra credits to graduate, and the following course was listed in the Italian Department: "132-385: The Italian Futurist Movement (3 credits, given in English)." It was taught by a Romanian-born woman named Ioana Georgescu. Dr Georgescu, as it turned out, had solid avant-garde credentials: she had mixed with the Neoist movement, an amalgamation of all avant-garde isms. Neoism was started at the tail end of the punk era by the Montreal-based Hungarian-Canadian artist Istvan Kantor, aka "Monty Cantsin." Ioana and Istvan were still friends—at the time he was promoting some of her performance pieces in Canada and post-communist Eastern Europe, including one called "Multilingual Manifesto: Smoked Tongue." They were part of a series called "Wound Art": there was a lot of smeared blood and screaming involved.

Ioana helped me to see the manifesto as a living thing and not just a thing of the past. During the 6-week summer course she traced the radical avant-garde that descended from Futurism through Dada and Surrealism to Lettrism and Fluxus and Situationism, and to post-punk movements like Neoism. In our daily meetings she revealed a degree of permissiveness that we had not previously encountered as undergraduates. There were no lectures; our classes consisted of heated discussions about art. Our only assignment was to invent an avant-garde movement with a video or performance piece and a manifesto. One student, a theater major named John, declaimed his manifesto as a sort of strip tease, ending up completely nude—which was slightly uncomfortable given the restrictive confines of our basement classroom. He had scrawled the main tenets of his manifesto in Sharpie across his chest and limbs. It was a long time ago but I think he even wrote something on his penis—none of us had the courage to stare at it long enough to read the words. My project with three other students was something called Aeroism, which involved Speedos and swimming caps and a Super 8 film we shot on the roof of my building in which we pretended to fly. It was stupid, completely ridiculous—and I knew instantly that I had found my people and my mode of expression.

From this start in Montreal I ran through a string of encounters with the manifesto as I moved through various cities over the next decade. I discovered the University of Iowa's renowned International Dada Archive, founded in 1979 in the middle of a corn field, during an otherwise unhappy year in Iowa City. In Dublin the mystical weirdness of William Butler Yeats was revealed to me, and I read all the plans and proclamations he made with Lady Gregory for the Abbey Theatre. From Dublin I moved to Madrid, where I spent my days off at the Reina Sofía soaking up avant-garde history. Then, unable to find a better job than part-time English teaching, I started a PhD at the University of Glasgow and discovered the American painter James McNeill Whistler, author of *The Gentle Art of Making Enemies* (1890), a collection of incendiary pamphlets and punitive legal actions. In Whistler's correspondence, which included letter wars with Oscar Wilde, I saw the antecedent of Ezra Pound and Wyndham Lewis, whose Vorticist movement would unsettle London a generation later. I discovered their manifesto-filled magazine *BLAST*, a "puce monster" that was too large to shelve, in a facsimile edition stocked at the branch of Waterstone's bookshop where I worked. Later I moved to Lisbon, where friends turned me on to Fernando Pessoa and the wild manifestos he wrote under various heteronyms. My last move was to the remote Portuguese island of Madeira, where I took a job at an interactive technologies institute. By necessity this job converted me from a Luddite who still wrote letters in longhand and didn't own a smart phone into a lapsed Luddite with a bit more knowledge of the digital world—knowledge that has helped me to discover and trace the rebirth of the manifesto in digital form.

All this time I wrote manifestos of my own. I wooed my future wife in our whirlwind courtship with a manifesto of love. Shamelessly—and perhaps a bit oddly, in retrospect—I cribbed it from *The Founding and Manifesto of Futurism*. It was called *The First Manifesto of Amorisme*. And did it work? It certainly did. It had the same scorching effect on my beloved that the first Futurist manifesto must have had on readers in 1909. She wrote me back with an even more incendiary manifesto, so hot my fingers were singed as they touched the page. A few months later we were married.

Manifestos are dark and powerful magic. They are personal as well as political. I love manifestos because they are brave but also vulnerable, fleeting, transient, constantly shifting, reinventing. They represent new starts, blank slates, big dreams and fierce masks. They call to mind a line from Chris Kraus's novel *I Love Dick* (1997): "we're all potentially bigger people than we are." They announce themselves the way I do in each new city I try to make my home, always feeling out of place yet trying to be bold in my difference.

Like most expats I live an imaginary life, a dream in the present borrowed against an uncertain nightmare of a future. Having escaped what Wyndham Lewis called the "sanctimonious icebox" of Canada—sublime nature tamed by a quietist culture—I wander Europe, owning nothing but books. I have no plans for the future—no house, no savings, no tenure. Instead I keep inventing myself in the present, living as well as I can from year to year, observing history in the making, trying to join in and lend a hand where I see a chance. To me manifestos represent the unity of thinking, doing and being. As Sara Ahmed writes: "In the labor of making manifest we make a manifesto."

Introduction

In March 1918, with the First World War still raging, the Dadaist Tristan Tzara laid down some rules for manifesto writing. He began: "To proclaim a manifesto you must want: ABC." As I write this book exactly a century later, what do I want? I want to understand how the manifesto, apparently a straightforward genre, can turn out to be so surprisingly complicated. I want to come up with a basic definition and some compelling examples. I want to discover how artists and activists are using the manifesto to respond to the current crisis. (Which crisis, you ask? I'll quote Marlon Brando: "What have you got?") I want to understand how the manifesto's return to prominence in the digital age might herald either a positive shift toward political engagement or a toxic slide into destructive upheaval and polarization, or both.

I want to ask a lot of questions. How did the genre develop? Why do manifestos look the way they do? How do you write one, and why would you want to? Why are they so bloody-minded? Why are they making a comeback in the age of "post-truth"? How do they relate to the broader digital culture, including its dark side? How does the art fit with the politics? Why are we all suddenly speaking in slogans and aphorisms? How can manifestos help us shape our future? How can they serve, in the words of French sociologist Bruno Latour, "Not as a war cry... but rather as a warning, a call to attention, so as to *stop* going further *in the same way* as before toward the future"? I want to find answers and share them with you, dear reader.

I should make it clear at the outset that when I say "manifesto" it refers to the revolutionary model—whether cultural or political—and not to the mainstream party platform (which it still denotes in the UK, for example). What was originally a form of authoritarian discourse used by kings and other tyrants underwent in the nineteenth century what Judith Butler might call a "subversive resignification." It became, in Marjorie Perloff's words, "the mode of agonism, the voice of those who are *contra*." In the digital world, manifestos have been there since the beginning: with the hackers, the cyberfeminists, the techno-utopians. They have got high art credentials—the manifesto is arguably the defining genre of modernism—but they've also always been "tainted" with politics and pop culture, the tricks of advertising and the desire for a mass audience. Which means they are right at home in our present post-everything era: of glitches and fake news, filter bubbles and context collapse.

A new wave of manifesto writing took off, post-9/11, as artists and activists began to wake up from the dreamlike apathy of the Clinton era. The tone of the 1990s, for a certain privileged population in the West, is perfectly captured in Ottessa Moshfegh's novel *My Year of Rest and Relaxation* (2018), in which the protagonist uses drug-induced sleep to "hibernate" from her life. This in turn recalls the "tranquillized Fifties" captured in Robert Lowell's poem "Memories of West Street and Lepke," the Eisenhower era of complacency that preceded the radical upheavals of the 1960s and the accompanying wave of movements and manifestos (civil rights, second-wave feminism, neo-avant-garde). After the successive ruptures of the 2008 financial crisis and the 2016 US presidential election, the manifesto is currently having its third major "moment." Manifestos have once again become part of the media atmosphere of everyday life, as they were before and after the First World War and again during the Vietnam War.

The avant-garde manifesto is a sort of *Through the Looking-Glass* reflection of the more common strangeness of the political manifesto. It is a genre that blends revolutionary zeal, dramatic performance and an insatiable thirst for novelty to create a singularly charismatic and circus-like delirium. Who is not electrified upon first reading *The Founding and Manifesto of*

Futurism (1909), the rant that launched a thousand imitators? Marinetti, Futurist-in-chief, summed up his manifesto formula in two key words: "violence and precision." The avant-garde manifesto channeled the anarchic energy of the new century into a literary form that was seductively strong and thrillingly direct. Now the manifesto has resurfaced online—ready once again to focus our energy and fight our cultural and political battles. For the Left this means using manifestos to imagine better futures; for the Right it means reaction and nostalgia for an imaginary past.

All manifestos are in some sense distorted and extreme. They are wish-lists of the overly ambitious, the public dreams of private Napoleons. This is especially true of the avant-garde manifesto. As the P. T. Barnum of the art world, the self-proclaimed "caffeine of Europe" (following Nietzsche's "I am dynamite"), Marinetti's manifestos influenced avant-gardes from Russia to Portugal and around the world. This is not to suggest that people actually *liked* Marinetti—in fact many claimed to despise him and his movement, sneering at his unbridled enthusiasm for technology. But Marinetti threw the switch that electrified the pre-war avant-garde. Whether or not you subscribed to his beliefs—not that he cared if you did!—his mania for transformation was contagious. The incendiary manifestos he and the other Futurists wrote soon spread like wildfire throughout Europe and across the Atlantic.

Manifestos are *refreshingly biased*. They have no false claims to objectivity, and neither will this book. Neutrality is antithetical to the manifesto, which is not only polemical, but (following avant-garde tradition) often proudly unreasonable as well. In the case of the avant-garde, this unreason is sometimes taken to the point where disruption and chaos, and unsettling the status quo, are more important than the principles or platforms they supposedly exist to promote. Manifestos can introduce new ways of thinking—sometimes in strange and extreme packages like the *SCUM Manifesto*, or for that matter *The Communist Manifesto*.

Manifestos make visible, they bring urgent causes to light, which is why they seem so timely in the age of movements like Black Lives Matter and #MeToo. They also seem current because they channel righteous anger.

It is important to keep in mind that manifestos are mere vessels, they can be about or promote anything, big or small, abstract or particular, good or bad. The paradox at the heart of the manifesto, to my mind, is that while *I* read manifestos to get new ideas and different perspectives on the world, to discover possible futures and different ways of acting and organizing and being, each manifesto in itself is just *one* way, one perspective—and worse yet, not always but often, it is a limited perspective. It's as if the person or the group writing it hasn't bothered to read hundreds of other manifestos as I have, but only wants to admit the existence of one. (This may of course be intentional on the part of the polemicist.) Manifestos may often resemble isolated bubbles unto themselves, but read together *en masse* they support the opposite of bubble thinking—you can't help but see the plurality and diversity of human thought.

I'm a manifesto omnivore: I devour all types of manifestos, except the truly horrific ones. Anything with a bit of wit or inspiration, on any subject, I love. Give me your Futurism, your Dada, your SCUM, your 95 Theses, your Ten Commandments. What do I find attractive in these texts that are often so clearly delusional, so irrational, so bossy, so aggressive? I love them for their energy and their flaws: they are confident, charismatic, swaggering, charming—they are all action, even when they're all talk. I'm writing this book in the summer of 2018, in the midst of fierce public debate on any number of topics. Every day seems to bring a new Armageddon. The manifesto strikes me as a symbol of this Age of Extremes—an age that prefers not to convince but to *convict* (as Whistler said). What do we lose when we abandon due process? What if the process is so broken that a revolution is needed? Should caution be damned? These are questions the manifesto asks.

Do manifestos bring about change? Yes—by presenting alternative visions, and in some cases outlining concrete actions. By making it clear that the status quo is no good, it's insufferable, intolerable, ridiculous. Manifestos are the first stop for visionaries. The avant-garde being by its very nature ahead of its time, many ideas now coming into the mainstream have been the subject of manifestos for ages. Eco-manifestos began in seventeenth-century England with the Diggers, and workers' rights with the Levellers. LGBTQ rights are championed in the manifesto of the Gay Liberation Front (1971), formed after the Stonewall riots, and *Queers Read This* (1990), which proclaimed during New York Pride at the height of the HIV/AIDS crisis: "An army of lovers cannot lose." Mina Loy wrote about escaping the shackles of biological determinism and traditional marriage to embrace something very like polyamory in her *Feminist Manifesto* in 1914. *UpWingers: A Futurist Manifesto* (1973) by FM-2030, the *Transhuman Manifesto* (1982) by Natasha Vita-More and the *Manifesto of Carnal Art* (1989) by Orlan all describe different forms of transhumanism—as do the manifestos of the Russian Cosmists in the early twentieth century. Accelerationism? Marshall McLuhan described the "acceleration of evolution" in 1969, in his Vorticist-inspired post-media manifesto *Counterblast*. Scanning the horizon, critiquing the present and pushing forward new futures are the manifesto's tasks. Many of the dreams first articulated in manifestos keep recurring: down through the decades, even centuries.

However, if provocation is the principal mode of the manifesto, and utopian dreams are its content, failure might be its most inevitable outcome. As Joyce Carol Oates reported in her classic essay "Notes on Failure" (1982): "When it was observed to T. S. Eliot that most critics are failed writers, Eliot replied: 'But so are most writers.'" (The English writer Quentin Crisp once quipped: "If at first you don't succeed, failure may be your style.") The failure rate of manifesto writing is much higher than average, since manifesto writers are working in a performative space in which words are often forced, against the odds, "to do things"—as the British philosopher J. L. Austin described it in a series of Harvard lectures published in 1962 as *How to Do Things with Words*. Doing things with words, especially making things happen in the world through sheer force of rhetoric (what Austin calls "perlocutionary effects") is hard work. It's not so bad if you are following one of Austin's simpler examples, such as ordering a meal or consenting to marriage ("I do"). But then you take, say, Valerie Solanas's *SCUM Manifesto* (1967), with its opening injunction to "overthrow the government, eliminate the money system, institute complete automation and eliminate the male sex." What if no one answers your call to action? Even proclaiming your intentions or making vows is a risky business. "We will glorify war...militarism, patriotism...beautiful ideas worth dying for," Marinetti famously proclaimed in 1909. These words might have been compelling after decades of peace and complacency—but not in 1918, after 4 years of unprecedented carnage in the name of "beautiful ideas."

There is a sadness about many manifestos, a whiff of desperation, a sense of belatedness and hopelessness. The last century is littered with manifestos full of broken promises and failed dreams. The historian Tom Holland recently tweeted: "The average house price on St George's Hill, where the Diggers in 1649 embarked on their experiment in running land as 'a common treasury for all', is apparently £3 million." The Diggers and Levellers pioneered incendiary rhetoric long before the revolutions of the nineteenth century, yet their once resonant words are falling on deaf ears as the concerns of the market dominate. Walter Gropius, in his founding manifesto for the Bauhaus art school in 1919, declared the noble aim of admitting "Any person of good repute, without regard to age or sex." But while enrolment of female students was initially high, Gropius soon began to limit their numbers, and women at the Bauhaus found themselves guided toward so-called "feminine subjects." Only a minority of manifestos actually end up marking the beginning of a path to full realization.

And then what if they succeed! For there is also the long history of manifesto dreams that turn into nightmares. But for all their (many and serious) failures, manifestos are, at their best, repositories of a kind of magic and madness that does not exist in any other genre. Take for example the Zaoum poets, who were an offshoot of Russian Futurism. If the Italian Futurists were bold and brash and stylish, the Russian Futurists, who cross-pollinated with Russian Formalists like Roman Jakobson, were mad geniuses and magicians with language. One Zaoum manifesto, *The Trumpet of the Martians* (1916) by Victor Khlebnikov, begins: "People of Earth, hear this!" Most manifestos are written from the point of view of disillusionment struggling back to hope: "hope not being hope," as Marianne Moore's poem "The Hero" (1932) states, "until all ground from hope has / vanished." Think of Shepard Fairey's *Hope* poster for Barack Obama's 2008 campaign: whatever the reality, the poster's single-word manifesto did bring hope back to politics after years of disillusionment. It summed up a platform and made a promise. It energized a voting public that wanted to believe that there was something more to politics than business as usual.

The singer Michael Jackson once wrote a manifesto, which the TV program *60 Minutes* discovered and aired in 2013. In 1979 Jackson laid out plans for his rebranding and subsequent world domination. He declared: "MJ will be my new name." In its highest form, the manifesto acts as a magic spell incanted by the visionary artist. It is a performative speech act that attempts to bring a new reality into existence. The most significant line in Jackson's manifesto is, "I will be magic." Manifesto writers over the past 2 centuries have tried, above all—to paraphrase

Marinetti and Oscar Wilde—to hurl their hopes at the stars, while lying, like most of us, in the muddy water of modernity's ditch. But to quote Beckett, whose characters are also fond of ditches, what manifesto writers can usually hope for is simply to "fail better" with each new campaign. And is it even a worthwhile fight?

Today we are all fluent in manifesto-ese. Our writing is not only rapid and concise but also confident and often arrogant. We throw out statements to an unseen and potentially limitless public. We aim to provoke sharp, immediate reactions that will be rewarded quantifiably with likes, retweets and other forms of instant feedback and rewards. We court engagement through witty aphorisms, calculated appeals to emotions, and striking visual images. Our intention is to elicit an immediate response from the reader, and our tactics are growing sharper every day. Our language on social media and even in private chat groups has become increasingly polemical, attention-seeking and extreme. We are led by Silicon Valley companies that seek to optimize engagement and shape habits—addiction that is literally engineered, wholly by design. We craft epigrams that are intended to shock, made to stand out in a sea of other bold declarations. If our quips are often couched in irony, this only makes our language more like the manifesto, not less. As one Vorticist manifesto declares: "We will convert the King if possible. A VORTICIST KING! WHY NOT?"

At the same time there is a growing—and very real—fear of public shaming, a zeitgeist captured in Jon Ronson's book *So You've Been Publicly Shamed* (2015). On Twitter and other social media platforms attacks are launched from the Left not only against reactionary voices but also against public figures (Margaret Atwood!) who are seen as being poor allies or somehow out of step with the political moment. This online behavior increasingly acts as a check on incendiary or even incautious speech. Recently we have seen both the strongest public speech in modern history—think of Samantha Bee calling the President's daughter a "cunt" on television—and the strongest public backlashes by so-called "snowflakes" against anything considered even slightly offensive from any ideological perspective. Welcome to the Age of Offense.

What can the manifesto do for YOU? It's a fair question. While it is true that manifesto writing is a healthy pastime that can prompt new ideas of all sorts by liberating you from the confines of careful speech and rational argument—that you really don't know what you stand for until you try to put your thoughts and beliefs into concise and convincing words—while that is all true, this book is not quite a writing guide, nor is it a DIY manual. Although my day job is at a university, this is also not an academic book. It is a handbook for activists, and a history for anyone who might be interested. It is written from a point of view of enthusiasm and engagement. It is, more often than not, a fan's notes. My hope is that after reading this book you will be so thoroughly steeped, so soaked to the skin, so infused with *manifestoism* that you will have no choice but to speak its language, at least for a little while.

I am writing this book as a manifesto handbook should be written: rapidly and rashly, with passionate conviction and not a lot of forethought. I am using as sources the stacks of yellowing manifestos that fill my office on the remote island where I live. If the bibliography seems slightly haphazard and eccentric, that's because it is: the mix of national origins in the editions reflects my nomadic life. I love collecting quotations, and manifestos are a wonderful source, so this book contains some of my favorites. I would be remiss if I didn't also call attention to the fact that this book draws examples mainly, though not exclusively, from Europe and North America. This is where the manifesto originally flourished, and this is what I happen to know best. But there are many, many examples of revolutionary and artistic manifestos from all over the world—born out of the spread of ideas over the past 2 centuries. I recommend the Penguin Modern Classics anthology *Why Are We "Artists"? 100 World Art Manifestos* (2017) as an entry point to the wealth of manifestos written outside the West, and I will discuss some of those examples here, alongside manifestos from movements seeking radical change and escape from hegemonic forces within the West.

If I delve too deeply into the content of these manifestos, if I try to compare mythologies, I'll quickly get lost. Instead I must stick to the form itself, the medium more than the message—but I can already anticipate that this will be a struggle throughout the book. I'm not an art historian, nor do I have any wish to recount the history of modern art (any more than you would wish to read it). This will be about the manifesto. All facts and opinions about art and politics—movements, ideologies and so on—will be incidental, ricochets off the central trajectory: how manifestos work, how they fail, why they exist, and why they continue to materialize in moments of crisis like the one we're living through right now. One more caveat: this book certainly does not contain all manifestos ever written; it may not contain your favorite manifestos, and it doesn't contain all of mine. I've included hundreds of manifestos—famous, unfamous and infamous—as illustrative examples in this book, but thousands more are waiting to be discovered and read. And written.

How to Write: A Manifesto

Listen!

There has never been a more perfect time to write a manifesto, or to be a manifesto writer.

NOW IS THE TIME.

But...**do it the hard way**. The hard way is good.

Why use a laptop when you can write longhand?

T. S. Eliot wrote: "The purpose of literature is to turn blood into ink."

Why use cold ink when you can use **your own hot blood?**

If you don't bleed writing it, the reader won't bleed reading it.

YOU WANT THE READER TO BLEED, DON'T YOU?

Make it newer.

And lo! How the craft of writing seems at times to have fallen, as our poor ignorant brethren follow corporate holograms through the heavily franchised city streets...yet how much there is still to write about, and more each day! How many ways of seeing! How many possible futures! How much ecstatic joy and beautiful sorrow still to express! Words, words! They fail us—always—and yet never!

Draw bold lines.

Then rub them out.

Confuse art with life.

Be at once frivolous and deadly serious.

Use alternate tunings. JAM A DRUMSTICK IN THE KEYS.

Forge the conscience of your race in the smithy of your soul. Then become distracted reading or having sex. Leave it in the smithy too long. Bring it out burnt. Scrape off the charred remains of the conscience of your race and publish it anyway. It will be better for the experience.

Pick a fight with Papa.

Stroke the belly of the underdog.

Write the manifesto you've always been destined to write, the one that uses every atom of your being, the one you've been waiting your whole life to write. **Repeat.**

Invent a new language.

Use no adverbs, or use only adverbs.

Discover language in rude and unexpected places.

Dig your sweetest words out of the dumpster behind the bakery.

James Joyce, for whom English was the language of the colonizer, wrote *Finnegans Wake* using at least 65 different languages. These included all the usual European suspects, Hebrew and Swahili, Arabic and Japanese, Sanskrit and Samoan, Chinese and Turkish, Basque and Persian, Esperanto and Volapük.

Don't hesitate to mess with the English.

WE WANT COURAGE, AUDACITY, AND REVOLT. (Without the Fascism.)

Build your own manifesto writing machine.

Rest the keyboard between your naked thighs.

Make your reader come; they'll always come back.

Make the page run red with raw animal heat.

CAUTION WILL GET US NOWHERE.

95 Theses on an Incendiary Form

Descriptions

1. To proclaim a manifesto...

...you must want: ABC, thunder against 1, 2, 3, lose your patience and sharpen your wings to conquer and spread a's, b's, c's little and big, sign, scream, swear, arrange the prose in a form of absolute and irrefutable evidence...Each page ought to explode, either from deep and weighty seriousness, a whirlwind, dizziness, the new, or the eternal, from its crushing humor, the enthusiasm of principles or its typographical appearance.

Tristan Tzara, Dada Manifesto (1918)

2. Ghost stories

"A specter is haunting Europe"—so begins one of history's most notorious ghost stories. It might seem odd to associate the manifesto, that most evidently nonfictional form, deeply rooted in serious legal and political matters, with fiction. But most manifestos, especially after *The Communist Manifesto*, start with some kind of preamble, and in that crucial opening section, if not in the demands that follow, a lot of storytelling happens. The preamble sets the scene, it provides context for the list of demands or principles that follows, and it snags our interest with a narrative hook. While their stated aim is to dispel the "nursery tale" of the specter of communism, in fact the absorbing ghost story told by Marx and Engels guarantees the reader's engagement through the more prosaic parts of the manifesto, like that eye-glazingly dull treatise on Socialist and Communist Literature.

3. Up all night

Another famous preamble is the "founding" part of *The Founding and Manifesto of Futurism*, the avant-garde manifesto that launched a thousand imitators. It begins with the rich and sensuously evocative line: "We had stayed up all night, my friends and I, under hanging mosque lamps with domes of filigreed brass, domes starred like our spirits, shining like them with the prisoned radiance of electric hearts." Marinetti spins a romantic tale of how the manifesto was written ("blackening reams of paper with our frenzied scribbling") and the movement founded—revealing the Decadent roots of the avant-garde. The breathless suspense and ecstatic imagery are used in part to draw the reader in, but they also create a rough picture of the new movement and the world it wants to overthrow ("the creaking bones of sickly palaces"). This origin narrative of Futurism includes a car chase (in 1909!) that ends with Marinetti crashing into a ditch and being hauled out by a group of fishermen. From that very spot, "faces smeared with good factory muck," their incendiary manifesto is proclaimed to Italy and the world.

4. Attention grabbing

The Futurists had a knack in their preambles for seizing the attention of the audience and creating legends to feed their own mythology. *Futurist Painting: A Technical Manifesto* (1910) begins with a breathless description of a violent brawl that took place at the live debut of their first manifesto:

> On the 18th of March, 1910, in the limelight of the Chiarella Theater of Turin, we launched our first manifesto to a public of three thousand people—artists, men of letters, students and others; it was a violent and cynical cry which displayed our sense of rebellion, our deep-rooted disgust, our haughty contempt for vulgarity, for academic and pedantic mediocrity, for the fanatical worship of all that is old and worm-eaten... The battle of Turin has remained legendary. We exchanged almost as many knocks as we did ideas, in order to protect from certain death the genius of Italian art.

5. Fight songs

People are wonderful. I love individuals. I hate groups of people. I hate a group of people with a "common purpose." Because pretty soon they have little hats. And armbands. And fight songs. And a list of people they're going to visit at 3am.
George Carlin

6. We

Traditionally manifestos were hardly ever issued by individuals. The Marxist historian Eric Hobsbawm drew attention to this fact during his appearance at the Manifesto Marathon held at the Serpentine Gallery in London in 2008. Hobsbawm was 91 years old at the time, having been conceived in Zurich when the Dadaists were declaiming manifestos in the Cabaret Voltaire. "I've been reading documents called manifestos for the best part of a century," he told the audience—starting at school in Weimar Berlin with *The Communist Manifesto*—and he went on:

> one thing that strikes me about [manifestos now] is that so many of them are individual statements and not, like almost all manifestos in the past, group statements, representing some kind of collective "we," formally organised or not. Certainly, that is the case of all political manifestos I can think of. They always speak in the plural.

One reason more manifestos are written by individuals these days, from a labor perspective, might be the rise to dominance of freelancing and startup culture. Just drop by a WeWork or a Starbucks and smell the manifestos brewing—combined with the smell of desperation in an atmosphere of increasing atomization and uncertainty.

7. One or two

Hobsbawm recognized that collective authorship has decreased with the rise of the internet. But why was the manifesto a group genre to begin with? Because it was a genre of solidarity, and there is strength in numbers. It was easy to throw a bunch of ideas into the ideological soup and give it a good stir. The truth behind the numbers implied by the collective "we," however, is a different matter. Just as on the internet nobody knows you're a dog, so if you start a movement nobody knows that you're actually just one lonely person sitting in a cafe. How many Dadaists, Futurists or Xenofeminists existed before the first manifesto was issued? Usually one or two. How many communists wrote *The Communist Manifesto*? Two—and mostly one.

8. Fake it till you make it

Near the end of his life, the Vorticist leader Wyndham Lewis admitted that although they were actually few, "It was essential that people should believe that there was a kind of army beneath the banner of the Vortex." Use the royal "we," he seems to suggest, and don't be too concerned about actual numbers. Fake it till you make it. If you build it, they will come. (If they don't come, try building something else.) But remember to be careful what you wish for: these days everyone is looking for a prophet, and the manifesto is a dangerously charismatic genre. A playful exercise in provocation may lead to the horror of actually being taken seriously! Then you'll find out whether you still have the strength of your loudly voiced convictions.

9. Collective tendencies

The poet Charles Baudelaire ridiculed the collective tendency of the literary vanguard. "This use of military metaphor," he wrote, referring to the term *avant-garde*, "reveals minds not militant but formed for discipline, that is, for compliance; minds born servile …which can only think collectively." It nevertheless remains true that whether your manifesto is composed individually or with a group, signatories will lend it weight. The list of signatories at the foot of a document can often be read like a map: a network drawing of the complex interactions and relations that make up a particular movement or scene, with the manifesto at the center as a connecting node. Eugene Jolas's Paris-based *transition* magazine published a manifesto called *The Revolution of the Word* in 1929 that was signed by no less than 16 people, a motley assortment of mostly American expatriates who aligned themselves with the avant-garde principles *transition* represented. Who actually writes a manifesto, in this sense, is beside the point. As in the case of the *Nouveau Réalisme Manifesto* (1960), written by the art critic Pierre Restany and designed by Yves Klein, the signatories "become conscious of their collective identity," their common cause—and unite to march arm in arm under the same banner.

10. How we live

Manifestos and little magazines are practical tools for achieving desired ends, which may include political ends. As the editors of *Légitime Défense*, a West Indian Marxist-Surrealist magazine, wrote in their 1932 manifesto: "If this little journal, a temporary instrument, breaks down, we shall find other instruments." So effective are these tools, in fact, that in many cases manifestos, carefully anthologized, and the ideas they express will outlast the movement itself, overshadowing its other achievements. The radical quasi-Situationist group King Mob, active in London in the late-1960s, whose principles (or anti-principles) survive in copies of the *King Mob Echo*, is one example. A manifesto slogan reads: "There is no longer any distinction between theory and action—politics is how we live." Conflating theory and action, saying and doing, is at the heart of the manifesto's performative nature—making words take action, all that blasting and blessing, cursing and damning and declaring—which is explained so neatly in Austin's *How to Do Things with Words* (1962). In the section of *The Gay Science* (1887) titled "Faced with a scholarly book," Nietzsche describes the relationship between ideas and experience in a way that closely mirrors the manifesto and its proximity to life, its valuing of action over lofty theoretical talk—and which also shows Nietzsche's influence on the energetic Marinetti: "our habit is to think outdoors, walking, jumping, climbing, dancing…Our first question about the value of a book, a person, or a piece of music is: 'Can they walk?' Even more, 'Can they dance?'"

11. Art and politics

The debate over the relationship between art and politics, and the role of politics in art, comes and goes from fashion much as the manifesto does, in regular waves. It has been revived most recently in the West under the Trump presidency, when some observers predicted a silver lining to the dark cloud that befell America: a boom in good, edgy art—art with sharp corners. The jury is still out on whether any such art has materialized. The art-and-politics debate usually centers on questions like: Is all art political? Does bad politics make good art? Is "political art" too focused on the pressures and concerns of the moment, to the detriment of timeless values? Putting that broader debate to one side, let's focus on the manifesto in particular—which is rooted in the political form, infused with the history of revolution and the struggle against all forms of oppression, and is thus always inescapably political. A lot of avant-garde manifestos are explicitly political: they want to change not just art but the whole world. In others the politics is more subtle. With the help of hindsight, Wyndham Lewis admitted reluctantly of Vorticism: "It may in fact have been politics. I see that now. Indeed it must have been. But I was unaware of the fact."

12. Taking sides

In 1937 the *Left Review* published a pamphlet edited by Nancy Cunard, *Authors Take Sides on the Spanish War*, in which 148 writers were surveyed and categorized by their responses "for," "against" or "neutral" to "the legal Government and the People of Republican Spain." The survey question itself was a pro-Republican manifesto, which made reference to scenes of "murder and destruction by Fascism" in Germany and Italy and insisted "it is impossible any longer to take no side." Unsurprisingly most were for the Left. Even the politically shy Samuel Beckett sent in the single-word manifesto: ¡UPTHEREPUBLIC! The handful of pro-Nationalist supporters included reactionaries like Evelyn Waugh, with 16 statements of fence-sitting (or general disgust) by H. G. Wells, Vita Sackville-West, Ezra Pound, T. S. Eliot and others filed under "neutral." In the 1930s Eliot in particular found himself out of step with the prevailing fashion for political extremes. His response states: "While I am naturally sympathetic, I still feel convinced that it is best that at least a few men of letters should remain isolated, and take no part in these collective activities." Lately we have swung back to an era of engagement, of taking sides, when to remain silent is increasingly seen not as being neutral or aloof but as complicit.

13. Making enemies

There have always been pockets of resistance to the manifesto's political side. Two aesthetes in late-nineteenth century London — the American artist James McNeill Whistler and the Irish poet and playwright Oscar Wilde — wrote proto-modernist manifestos in which they tried hard to shun politics entirely, being all for *l'art pour l'art*. Whistler's "Ten O'Clock" lecture of 1885, published as an elegant pamphlet in 1888 and then reprinted in *The Gentle Art of Making Enemies* (1890), told fashionable Londoners — Wilde himself was in the audience — to simply "leave art alone." It was of no concern to the public, he said, except in their role as passive consumers. Critics and educators, amateurs and dilettantes, "gentle priest[s] of the Philistines" — they could all get stuffed, in Whistler's view. Art was for artists, and should remain mysterious and elite, untouched by the masses, "the intoxicated mob of mediocrity." The public, Whistler argued, should not even be allowed to enter museums to look at art — a right that had been granted only relatively recently. "Why," he asked, "after centuries of freedom from it, and indifference to it, should it now be thrust upon them?"

14. Not so useless

Such a message, of course, *was* political. Wilde, whose manifestos include *The Poets and the People: By One of the Latter* (1887), had a more mixed and generally upbeat message. His Paterian aestheticism was tempered by the socialism of William Morris—in fact he was a target of Whistler, his onetime friend and neighbor in Chelsea, for his democratizing tendencies. In his most famous manifesto, the "Preface" to *The Picture of Dorian Gray* (1891), Wilde argues for artistic autonomy: "All art is quite useless." Yet Wilde's politics, progressive rather than reactionary, seep in through the cracks. By declaring, "It is the spectator, and not life, that art really mirrors," Wilde frees art from the function of realistic representation, opening the door to Symbolism and Expressionism. And by calling "vice and virtue" merely "materials" for the artist, Wilde attempts to liberate art from the shackles of Victorian morality. The fact that his actions led to the very literal iron shackles he wore for his art and sexuality only 4 years later (his own writings having been used in court to convict him of gross indecency, with a punishment of hard labor) adds rather a lot of weight to his seemingly light and flippant manifesto. Political, of course, can also mean personal. *"Tout est politique"* was a popular slogan during the demonstrations in France of May 1968. Or as Derek Jarman wrote of the sixties in his diary *Modern Nature*: "We were not apolitical: our agenda was personal."

15. No apologies

In one sense the manifesto's political history is liberating. Unlike fiction or poetry, the manifesto is natively and (for the most part) unapologetically political. Rather than politicizing art, the manifesto aestheticizes politics. The German critic Walter Benjamin took Italian Futurism strongly to task for this potentially fascistic move (and in fairness, Marinetti's Futurists did flirt briefly with Mussolini's Fascists). The critique comes in the epilogue to his essay "The Work of Art in the Age of Mechanical Reproduction," where Benjamin argues that "Fascism is the introduction of aesthetics into political life," and that Futurism's glorification of war, imperialism and military technology supports this Fascism. In a description that could easily apply to late capitalism, Benjamin writes: "Fascism sees its salvation in giving these masses not their right, but instead a chance to express themselves." He adds, returning us to the start of this theme, that "the artistic gratification [through the spectacle of war] of a sense perception that has been changed by technology…is evidently the consummation of *l'art pour l'art*" — that is, humanity has become "self-alienated" to the extent "that it can experience its own destruction as an aesthetic pleasure of the first order." Not where Wilde wanted to end up, perhaps. But Benjamin's words should set off alarm bells in our own age, which is witnessing the mediated spectacle of environmental collapse on a planetary scale.

16. Size matters

How short is too short? Do we need to distinguish between a manifesto and a "minifesto"—a category coined by the Portuguese Marxist scholar Boaventura de Sousa Santos in his book *Epistemologies of the South* (2014)? What about "tiny manifestos" of the sort included in David Graeber's *Fragments of an Anarchist Anthropology* (2004)? Where do slogans fit in—like the iconic poster from the 1960s that combines an image of Malcolm X peering out of the window holding an M1 semi-automatic rifle with the text: "Liberate Our Minds—By Any Means Necessary"? It has both a clear message and a call to action. Or Ezra Pound's oft-repeated dictum, "Make it new," which captures the spirit of a movement (modernism, broadly defined) and exhorts the reader to act. Or what about *"sic semper tyrannis"*—"death to tyrants"—shouted by John Wilkes Booth as he shot President Lincoln at Ford's Theatre in Washington, DC on Good Friday, 1865? Did the utterance carry enough performative weight to constitute a manifesto? Surely it did—has any other manifesto been so clear in its sentiment and so compelling in its execution? The Manson Family's scrawl of "Healter (sic) Skelter" in blood at the scene of the Tate/LaBianca murders in 1969 was another kind of phrasal manifesto, supposedly signaling the start of a revolution. Jean Arp's *Infinite Millimeter Manifesto* (1938), meanwhile, is (as the title suggests) both brief—compact, elliptical, allusive—and conceptually all-encompassing. It even manages in the space of a few lines to include the sort of denial common to "anti-manifestos": "I for one don't draw up a plan first as if I were dealing with a time-table, a calculation or a war." Nietzsche, the philosopher whose influence on the manifesto's outspoken and aphoristic style was more profound than any other except Marx, wrote: "it is my ambition to say in ten sentences what everyone else says in a book"—an admirable goal. A few years ago, *A Short Manifesto on the Future of Attention* was published by Michael Erard in the *Design Observer*, in which the author confronts the issue of short attention spans and the link to valuing commodities. Unfortunately, it was not short enough—my attention quickly wandered elsewhere.

17. A truly short manifesto

Better, obviously, is something like this: *A Short Manifesto* (1964) by the Dutch conceptual artist Stanley Brouwn. It ends with a vision of the future, in AD 4000:

> NO MUSIC
> NO THEATRE
> NO ART
> NO
> THERE WILL BE SOUND
> COLOR
> LIGHT
> SPACE
> TIME
> MOVEMENT

Or the *Laws of Sculptors* (1969), by the English artists Gilbert and George, written during the same decade of social upheaval but with a tone that rejected the surrounding chaos. In their manifesto, four concise laws are laid out, including: "Never worry assess discuss or criticize but remain quiet, respectful and calm."

18. Pure excess

Manifestos quickly lose their communicative effectiveness as their page count increases. Very long manifestos are usually the products of disturbed minds: think of Hitler's 700-page *Mein Kampf* (1925), the Unabomber Ted Kaczinski's 35,000-word *Industrial Society and Its Future* (1995) and more recently Norwegian mass murderer Anders Breivik's *2083: A European Declaration of Independence*. These interminably long manifestos try to impress by their sheer physical bulk—communication has little to do with it. On the other hand, part of the manifesto's iconoclastic nature is its tendency toward excess. There is surely nothing more excessive than going on a book-length rant and then drawing attention to your "manifesto" with a shooting rampage, an assassination, a bombing campaign or a world war. Valerie Solanas's *SCUM Manifesto* (1967) is a rare exception to the rule of longer-makes-duller, and is far and away the most readable example of the fanatical longform manifesto—Andy Warhol would have done well to give her a second chance. André Breton's *Manifesto of Surrealism*, published as a booklet on October 15, 1924, is another example of a longer manifesto that manages to stay on the right side of readability and (arguably) sanity. Breton's pleasantly meandering discourse goes beyond the average manifesto by providing examples of Surrealism in practice, rather than simply and succinctly laying out guiding principles. The excessive length may have been strategic, given that Breton was then fighting for control of the nascent movement and term "Surrealism" with the French-German poet Yvan Goll, who had published a shorter manifesto of Surrealism just 2 weeks earlier in the debut issue of *Surréalisme* magazine. Breton, however, won the battle with his longer and more authoritative treatise—a second issue of *Surréalisme* never appeared.

19. Be bold

I hope it is becoming clear by now that in manifestos there is no room for moderation. Think in slogans. Attack your rivals. Kill your idols. Go electric. This is the revolution. Donna Haraway's *A Cyborg Manifesto* (aka *Manifesto for Cyborgs*, 1985) starts with a note on the manifesto's playful style, and what that style lets you get away with: "Irony is about humor and serious play. It is also a rhetorical strategy and a political method, one I would like to see more honored within socialist-feminism. At the center of my ironic faith, my blasphemy, is the image of the cyborg." If you've read a lot of manifestos, Haraway's explanation may seem overly cautious. But in academia this was (and still is) pretty far-out stuff. As Cary Wolfe points out, *A Cyborg Manifesto* brought a "stylistic and rhetorical bravado" and a "swagger" to the ivory tower, unleashing "a new and unprecedented range of expression and experimentation for serious academic writing"—much as *The Founding and Manifesto of Futurism* did for artists at the beginning of the twentieth century, ripping down the curtains and opening all the windows in the house at once. Haraway's writing also has the virtue of substance. But her intervention would not have made the same impact in the form of a conventional academic essay. It required that combination of "violence and precision" to remain a benchmark of feminist and post-humanist scholarship several decades later.

20. We're America, bitch

Our language is beginning to shift toward the poetic, the aphoristic and the epigrammatic, thanks to constant nudging from technology. We are all producing shards of poetry and writing sharp little manifestos every time we message or post or tweet, instead of (what now seem like) the baggy expository monsters of the pre-digital age. From *BLAST* to Twitter there is a longstanding tendency to draw inspiration from the tabloid headline. Increasingly, acceleratingly, everything is becoming a scandal-sheet screamer: loud, blunt, outrageous, emotional, visceral, visual and direct. On the morning I'm writing this, two pieces of news from America have caught my eye. The first is that Robert De Niro won a standing ovation at the Tony Awards for repeatedly shouting "Fuck Trump!" And the second is that, when asked to define the Trump Doctrine, a senior White House official replied that the doctrine was: "We're America, bitch." Social media is teaching us to perform our outrage and desire in public in the most impactful—and some would say least articulate and most harmful—possible terms. Good or bad, this is a reflex that aligns well to manifesto writing, and says something about the manifesto's current vogue.

21. Language of desire

The first Futurist manifesto ends in an aggressive male fantasy: "Erect on the summit of the world...we hurl defiance to the stars!" But Valentine de Saint-Point's *Futurist Manifesto of Lust* (1913) goes even further, calling for a universal *new* sexuality based on raw desire, on "the attraction at once delicate and brutal between two bodies, of whatever sex." She declares: "WE MUST MAKE LUST INTO A WORK OF ART." What else is the manifesto but *lust as art*? Advertising teaches us that selling is not about needs but desires. Sex sells. If sex can sell soap, it can sell Surrealism. The language of desire is the best way to win converts. Guillaume Apollinaire once told poets: "you should compete with the labels on perfume bottles." At their most elemental, manifestos—like the advertisements they both ape and influence—are simply "machines to generate desire."

22. Not giving any recipes

"Advertising" derives from the Latin *advertere*, "to turn toward." This seems accurate but outdated—it harkens back to a time when advertising pitched actual products. Now it's the image that is for sale. At the height of the avant-garde a century ago, writers like Marinetti realized the medium *was* the message, embracing and pioneering new techniques for advertising. The message proper took on a secondary role, or became unintelligible, or disappeared altogether. "I am writing a manifesto and I don't want anything," as Tzara declared in 1918. Or, as he put it more succinctly the following year: "not being a vegetarian I'm not giving any recipes." Since the historical avant-garde, the manifesto has come to advertise only itself, or itself and its "ism." The ism is a brand, and the manifesto is a marketing tool. The ism, like all brands, acts as a guarantee of quality and consistency. It is a nexus of encoded values. Consumers of the ism can choose to buy into a particular cluster of values. Brand loyalty is sought. What is your artistic identity? Which ism are you? Are you a Futurist or an Imagist? Or is Dada more your thing? Aided by graphic design, the manifesto embodies the values of the movement just as a good advertisement embodies its brand. Marinetti's favorite lesson from advertising was the old adage: there's no such thing as bad press. He wrote about "the pleasures of being booed" and picked fights with audiences across Europe. Soon other isms followed his lead, using shock and outrage as their primary tactics. The exchange between the avant-garde and advertising is mutual. As Ian Bogost points out: "Today, revolution is the ultimate branding exercise. The operation of a product...is less important than the depth of its commitment to the rhetoric of innovation." With all advertisements, as with all ideologies, *caveat emptor*—let the buyer beware.

23. The crowded marketplace of isms

Clearing space for a new brand in a crowded marketplace isn't easy. Cutting through the noise and achieving "market differentiation" presents a constant challenge for marketing firms. Elements used to distinguish a brand from its competitors include novelty, slogans and visual appeal. The historical avant-garde offered a wealth of all three—one reason why the early twentieth century is still mined so heavily by graphic designers and advertising firms. Vorticism, for example, published only two manifesto-filled numbers of its magazine, *BLAST*. But in the art and design section of any good bookshop you can still find a facsimile edition of *BLAST*, whose lurid pink cover with the title emblazoned diagonally across it in oversized print still leaps out as fresh and eye-catching as it did in July of 1914. The real advertisements of 1914 must not have stood a chance against Vorticism's powerful campaign, which was defeated only by the military campaigns and even louder blasting of the First World War that began later that summer. In order to find space and mark out territory, avant-garde manifestos often attacked other movements, especially Futurism. Mocking Futurism's forays into fashion, one Vorticist manifesto declared: "We do not want to make people wear Futurist Patches, or fuss men to take to pink and sky-blue trousers." In a draft manifesto of *Sensationism*, written in English, the Portuguese writer Fernando Pessoa claimed that his ism—which he referred to as not quite "a movement" but more "an attitude"—embraced and synthesized all others: "extracting honey from all the flowers that have blossomed in the gardens of European fancy." Avant-garde movements expanded to take in all forms of artistic creation: poetry, music, sculpture, painting, theater. Futurism went farther than most by adding other facets of life, including fashion, cooking (a Futurist cookbook), politics (the ill-conceived partnership with Mussolini's Fascists) and architecture (still seen in the Futurist buildings of Asmara, the former colonial capital of Eritrea). But wait, you might say: does all this borrowing from the logic of capitalism and the methods of advertising and marketing threaten to commodify protest and co-opt true cultural and societal innovation? Well yes, certainly. That is a great risk. It's not easy to get outside capitalism these days—just ask the Black Bloc protesters taking selfies with their iPhones and posting them on Instagram.

24. Bright colors and a very large font

When the Vorticists published their magazine full of manifestos, it had óne word—*BLAST*—stamped across the bright pink cover. Inside it was all screaming tabloid headline typeface declaring: "BLAST First (from politeness) ENGLAND" and "OH BLAST FRANCE." The fact that *BLAST* contained some clever writing was almost beside the point. It was a visual provocation, a red rag to John Bull. The Italian Futurists and Russian Constructivists were among the first to play with typography in their manifestos, creating an explosive form to match the revolutionary content. The Futurist cry of *parole in libertà!*—words in freedom—was represented by scattershot typography in posters, pamphlets and artists' books like Marinetti's *Zang Tumb Tumb* (1914). The "Futurist Synthesis of the War," issued as a pamphlet in the first month of the war, drew up a plan of attack with a wedge of "Futurist" Allied Forces advancing on "Passéist" Axis Powers, not unlike the Russian El Lissitsky's famous propaganda poster *Beat the Whites with the Red Wedge* (1919). Apollinaire's "calligrammes" (1913-16)—a sort of visual or concrete poetry—were also influential, and some may be read as manifestos in themselves. "Cheval" declares: "Give yourself up to this art where the sublime does not exclude charm and brilliancy does not blur the nuance it is now or never the moment to be sensitive to poetry for it dominates *all dreadfully*." Dada built upon all of these innovations.

25. By any means necessary

In the second-wave avant-garde of the 1960s the visual tricks of the earlier movement were recycled and expanded, and shock tactics were even more pervasive. The Fluxus Manifesto (1963) used handwritten capital letters, interspersed with blocks of type, when it called on readers to "PROMOTE A REVOLUTIONARY FLOOD AND TIDE IN ART." All capital letters were also used in the tabloid-style *King Mob Echo* (1968-9), the magazine of the London offshoot of Situationism. The King Mob manifesto *We Are Outlaws* (1968), whose ransom note design was later used by Jamie Reid in his cover artwork for the Sex Pistols, is sprinkled with the all-caps "BAMN," the acronym for the slogan "By Any Means Necessary" popularized by Malcolm X. The Black Panther manifesto of 1970, in poster form, was dominated by the arresting image of leader Bobby Seale strapped to an electric chair, with the headline: "The Fascists Have Already Decided in Advance to Murder Chairman Bobby Seale in the Electric Chair" (a reference to the 1969 Chicago Conspiracy Trial). During the same period the Situationists in France used comic strips, photo collages and street art to get their message heard and attract people to the fight. Fame feeds on controversy. Great artists are great self-advertisers. The manifesto is the message, and the most direct route to the brain is from the image to the eye. Yves Klein knew it. In fact it is amazing that any artist would think a plain text is ever enough to cut through the noise of modernity. When the manifesto of *Nouveau Réalisme* was published in 1960, it was painted in the patented International Klein Blue (IKB), the same vivid blue that electrified his monochrome paintings and his copies of the *Venus de Milo* and the *Winged Victory of Samothrace*, the blue that adorned the naked bodies of women he used as "live brushes" for his Anthropometry paintings. Two years earlier Klein had gone so far as to write a letter to President

Eisenhower outlining his plans for a "Blue Revolution"—a manifesto for a utopian society based on the principles of the French Revolution, but without the capitalism. The details, unfortunately, were somewhat vague. Can a manifesto omit words altogether? Yes: the Portuguese artist Paula Rego did it in her painting *Manifesto for a Lost Cause* (1965), and there are many other examples—although it helps if you call it a manifesto in the title.

26. Performance

Visuals are important, but so is the whole *event*. A manifesto must be launched in a style that makes it memorable. Marinetti delayed the Italian publication of the first Futurist manifesto after an earthquake struck Sicily on January 2, 1909, killing 200,000 people. There was no room for Futurism on the front page that week. But the delay gave him a better idea: in February he traveled to Paris, capital of the art world, where he published the manifesto on the front page of *Le Figaro*. The Futurists threw their manifestos off balconies, dropped them from airplanes and hurled them out of speeding cars. Why not, for that matter, write your manifesto in blood, or paint it on a naked body? Push it through the wire mesh window of a police truck, or leave it behind the barricades. Shortly before he was assassinated in Mexico by Stalin's agent Ramón Mercader, Leon Trotsky declared in *Towards a Free Revolutionary Art* (with André Breton and Diego Rivera, 1938): "never has civilization been menaced so seriously as today." How true that prophetic line turned out to be! Both for the outbreak of the Second World War and more personally for Trotsky and his unfortunate encounter with the ice pick. And what a story!

27. Pantomime fisticuffs

The manifesto is a performative genre and drama is inscribed in its history. Over-the-top performances are part of what give manifestos their feeling of danger and magic. The underground theater has long been associated with manifestos. *SCUM Manifesto* author Valerie Solanas's dramatic shooting of Andy Warhol in 1968 when he lost the only copy of her play, *Up Your Ass*, is one example of the frequent forays manifestos make across the lines of text and performance. Shortly after her arrest, Solanas's friends in the New York theater collective Up Against the Wall, Mother Fucker staged a "happening" to try (unsuccessfully) to attract support for her defense. Performance is part of the manifesto's materiality, its existence in the world. Marinetti made art into a kind of Punch and Judy show, full of pantomime fisticuffs and bold, simple story lines: destroy the past, embrace the future. From Dada manifestos in the Cabaret Voltaire in 1916 to Antonin Artaud's manifestos for a *Theater of Cruelty* to the radical street theater of the 1960s to Lars von Trier's scattering of red leaflets, printed with his *Vow of Chastity*, into the audience at a Paris cinema conference on the future of film in 1995, the manifesto—*manu festus*, "struck by hand"—has always been about striking gestures.

28. Wear a mask

Figuratively, that is, not literally (unless it helps). Put on a face that is bold and charismatic. When you write a revolutionary manifesto your persona should be extroverted, verging on sociopathic. The shy, bookish Fernando Pessoa let his gregarious "heteronym" Álvaro de Campos write his most incendiary manifesto, "ULTIMATUM," published in *Portugal Futurista* in 1917. "ULTIMATUM" begins as a series of shouts: "Get out!" (*Fora!*) Wearing his mask of assertive confidence, the young poet tells all the old guard of Europe their time is up, from Anatole France to Rudyard Kipling. "Out out out!" he shouts. "Clean all this crap from out of my sight! Out with all of you! Out!" Like Pessoa, the introspective William Butler Yeats (whose name appears on Pessoa's list) donned the masks of various public selves that allowed him to speak freely and unselfconsciously. Oscar Wilde espoused "The Truth of Masks" in *Intentions* (1891), his book of aesthetic manifestos. Once he gave up Vorticism and other collective activities, the anti-social Wyndham Lewis simply called himself The Enemy, vanishing forever behind his mask. Nowadays writing from behind an aggressive mask is a common feature of social media culture. Glenn Greenwald, for example—best known for his role in bringing to light Edward Snowden's disclosures about government surveillance in 2013—has been described as having an "offline openness to rebuttal" which is in stark contrast to his behavior on Twitter, described by a fellow journalist as "bloodlust and sarcasm."

29. Despot and revolutionary

As a manifesto writer you are caught in an impossible dilemma; a contradiction exists at the very core of the genre. On one hand, the manifesto is authoritarian, pushy and humorless. It seeks to impose its will on the listener or reader. But it can also be anti-authoritarian, free-spirited, silly and ironic. It questions everything and obeys nothing except itself—sometimes not even that. Dada, replete with self-negation, is one example. And Futurism? Should we take the poet-dandy who calls himself the "caffeine of Europe" seriously when he tells us to "set fire to the library shelves," or to hold Futurist banquets in "tactile pajamas" and eat "polyrhythmic salad"? Manifestos must be completely serious or no one will take them seriously; yet they must also admit that, on some level, they are utterly ridiculous and no one *should* take them seriously. How do you feel when you see a person who is red in the face, screaming with self-righteous indignation or rage, utterly unaware of their own absurdity? The spectacle is engrossing, disturbing—but ultimately laughable. Caught in a contradiction, playing both despot and revolutionary, artist and critic, "straight man" and clown, the manifesto writer must persevere. The secret to this perseverance is drama. The theater of the absurd. You build a little self-contained world and invite the audience in. Describe this world in detail. Don't be afraid to make it entertaining. The more compelling the illusion, the more willing the convert.

30. Lists

When you come to the list—of principles, threats or demands—it is best to use numbers: they are eye-catching and get right to the point. Make it a round number, like five or ten or 20. Or don't— why follow rules? Manifestos are primarily about change. Rules are made to be twisted, mocked, overturned and burned like so many parked cars. Centuries ago, manifestos were used to issue declarations of war on neighboring kingdoms. Take this as your model. Declare war on your opponent. Speak like a monarch. Stick to your principles—the big points. Don't get hung up on details, which must be negotiated *after* the battle is over. The list of principles or demands is the most recognizable feature of the manifesto. *The Communist Manifesto* has a conventional list of ten "measures" in the second section. The original 1966 Black Panther Party manifesto is a "Ten-Point Program" that imports and recontextualizes large sections of the *Declaration of Independence* ("We hold these truths to be self-evident, that all men are created equal"). When the German industrial designer Dieter Rams published his list of "good design" principles in the 1970s, a list that has strongly influenced Apple design, the list came to a neatly rounded ten points. Being prone to excess, the list in the first Futurist manifesto—like the amplifier in *This is Spinal Tap*—goes up to 11. The Situationists' *Theses on the Paris Commune* (1962) comprises 14 points. Because the numbered list is so recognizable as a feature, it is here that one feels most strongly the sense of *belatedness*—the ironic distance, the repeated performance, the debt to past revolutions. The format has been *de rigueur* since at least as far back as the *Declaration of the Rights of Man* (1789), not to mention Martin Luther's 95 *Theses* (1517), nailed to the door of All Saints' Church in Wittenberg, Saxony, 5 centuries ago, or indeed the Ten Commandments that lie at the center of Judaism and Christianity. But despite this

long history the list of numbered tenets feels contemporary—
it conveys a sense not of fusty tradition but of straight talk
and an urgent need for action. In fact, the list is one reason
why manifestos feel so modern: viewed online, they are easily
mistaken for "listicles" and other ubiquitous forms of internet
clickbait.

31. More lists

Manifesto lists come in many styles and formats. They range from the straightforward "ten commandments" to lists in columns, similar to the "pro-con" lists people draw up to make difficult decisions. For the past decade the speculative designers Anthony Dunne and Fiona Raby have kept an updatable A/B list on their website as a "work in progress" — where "A" includes mainstream commercial design terms, and "B" suggests reinterpretations, redefinitions and corrections: so "affirmative" becomes "critical," "consumer" becomes "citizen," "makes us buy" becomes "makes us think" and so on. The Vorticists used this format in their eccentrically English "blast" and "bless" lists, featuring the names of friends, revolutionary leaders, celebrities, local businesses, consumer products and plenty of inside jokes from the London art scene. Among the blasted are the French philosopher Henri Bergson, the British Academy, the Lyceum Club, the English cricketer C. B. Fry, cod liver oil and the Post Office; blessed are the Pope, Charlotte Corday (the assassin of French revolutionary Jean-Paul Marat), Oliver Cromwell, James Joyce, caster oil and Madame Strindberg, the estranged wife of playwright August Strindberg and owner of a notorious London nightclub, much frequented (and decorated) by the Vorticists, called The Cave of the Golden Calf. Most eccentrically of all, some items are blasted *and* blessed: these include England, France and humor. Before *BLAST* there was Apollinaire — who was always first in everything — and his manifesto *"L'Antitradition-futuriste"* (1913), which declared *"merde"* to the past, to critics, to professors, to museums and to the other usual targets of Futurism (though strangely also to the proto-modern poets Whitman and Baudelaire), and *"rose"* to friends and fellow travelers like Marinetti and the Futurists, Picasso, Matisse, Duchamp, Delaunay, Picabia — and most of all, to Apollinaire himself.

32. Still more lists

Maggie Nelson's genre-defying book *Bluets* (2009) is made up of 240 numbered sections, many of them only one or two lines long. Is this a manifesto? It certainly represents a bold new way of writing, and possibly of desiring and living. A blue manifesto, or a manifesto of the blues? Sure, why not? (Think of Yves Klein.) Then again, lists also suggest constraint, restraint. Reining in our behavior. Putting a lid on it, policing it. Down with that sort of thing. The sixth Dogme 95 "Vow of Chastity" states: "The film must not contain superficial action. (Murders, weapons, etc. must not occur.)" The designers Charles and Ray Eames did a famous Q&A in 1972, not unlike a manifesto, where they described design as "The sum of all constraints." When asked in a follow-up question, "Does Design obey laws?" they answered by asking: "Aren't constraints enough?" Coming up with new constraints, as manifestos often do, is one way of breaking out of old habits. In this sense rules are freeing rather than constricting. The *Ghent Manifesto* (2018), a manifesto for a "city theater of the future," is one example. Its ten rules encourage public engagement, the use of non-professionals, crossing language and national borders, and staging performances in conflict zones. Constraints like these nudge us to leave our comfort zones. Constraint-based manifestos are vastly preferable, I think, to prohibition-based "Thou shalt not" manifestos. In the end a manifesto is a kind of recipe. Marcel Duchamp used to enjoy giving out recipes, including a famous one for *steak tartare*, as well as instructions for his Readymades. The Italian Futurists produced an entire cookbook, along with the *Manifesto of Futurist Cuisine* (1930). Tzara said: "I'm not giving any recipes." Dada lists and repetition often resemble incantation more than instruction, as if the aim was not to teach a new way of doing but actually to make magic—to cast a spell.

33. Clarity, or a cautionary note

Lists are clear, and clarity is said to be a virtue—but is it always? Or is it sometimes just a dumbing down, and worse, is it not prone to authoritarianism? Manifestos are clear and decisive, or they sound like it. Hence their increasing attraction in a world of what David Foster Wallace called "Total Noise," the overwhelming stimulus of contemporary life and the feeling that we're never getting on top of all the information available (because we're not). DFW was writing in 2007, the year the new media age was just getting started with the iPhone, Twitter, Tumblr, Netflix and so on. No wonder a book like *12 Rules for Life* (2018) by Jordan Peterson, with its accompanying YouTube lectures and endless spin-offs—a book with little to offer but the consoling illusion of clarity—can sell millions of copies in the space of a few months.

34. Fleeting

The poet Frank O'Hara gives us the best example of the manifesto as a fleeting, momentary impulse. O'Hara wrote *Personism: A Manifesto* (1959) in less than an hour, at the request of his editor Donald Allen (who was already on his way across town to pick it up). It is a humorous mock-manifesto that is nonetheless, like so many others, still a manifesto proper:

> Personism has nothing to do with philosophy, it's all art. It does not have to do with personality or intimacy, far from it! But to give you a vague idea, one of its minimal aspects is to address itself to one person (other than the poet himself)...It was founded by me after lunch with LeRoi Jones on August 27, 1959, a day in which I was in love with someone (not Roi, by the way, a blond). I went back to work and wrote a poem for this person. While I was writing it I was realizing that if I wanted to I could use the telephone instead of writing the poem, and so Personism was born. It's a very exciting movement which will undoubtedly have lots of adherents.

The manifesto embodies O'Hara's casual spoken style as well as his serious convictions, lightly worn, about art and poetry— all perfectly captured in the rapid throwaway method of its composition. The Free City movement of the 1960s in San Francisco encouraged its followers to reuse its newspaper, which contained a number of manifestos, in creative ways: "Use this paper to start a fire or for toilet paper; tear it up for confetti and celebrate the free city; use it to start a revolution. Wad it up and throw it at your lover." If manifestos can survive the immediate moment of their dissemination, they often end up caught in the tension between their status as throwaway statements and their use as historical documents. Futurist manifestos were ephemeral, hurled off balconies and out of speeding automobiles, but like many similar documents they have since been carefully archived, translated, anthologized and reproduced in textbooks of art history, literature, politics, architecture and rhetoric.

35. NOW

D. H. Lawrence once wrote a poem he called "Manifesto" (1916), which ends:

> We shall not look before and after.
> We shall *be, now*.
> We shall know in full.
> We, the mystic NOW.

Now, the present—even, ironically enough, in Futurist manifestos—is the native timeframe of the manifesto. The manifesto is about now, this fleeting moment, this world, what's happening around us. Like journalism, manifestos are caught in the daily trench warfare of the present, making only occasional glances above the parapet at the wider arc of history. Their rhetoric, of course, does not always reflect this: manifestos often begin with sweeping histories. But their real concern is with the fight *now*, whether for art, or politics, or both. Like Auden's "Spain" (1937), that great poem of the Spanish Civil War, everything is put on hold until the present battle is won:

> To-morrow for the young the poets exploding like bombs,
> The walks by the lake, the weeks of perfect communion;
> To-morrow the bicycle races
> Through the suburbs on summer evenings. But to-day the struggle.

Provocations

36. A little violence

The artist Jenny Holzer is best known for two serial works which show a debt to the manifesto: *Truisms* (1977-9) and *Inflammatory Essays* (1979-82). Both have appeared across numerous media over the past few decades, including marquees in New York's Times Square, but they are most striking in their original context: as simple posters, pasted up and peeling off walls around the city, their often shocking messages available to be seen and read by anyone passing by. In an interview from 1989 Holzer says that she felt drawn to the genre because it was "uneasy and hot" and she "wanted things to really flame." She describes two sides of manifesto writing, both of which relate to its use as a means of provocation. On one hand there is "the scary side where it's an inflamed rant" — the side captured in a "truism" like: "VIOLENCE IS PERMISSIBLE EVEN DESIRABLE OCCASIONALLY." Then there is "the positive side, when it's the most deeply felt description of how the world should be," like: "REVOLUTION BEGINS WITH CHANGES IN THE INDIVIDUAL." But Holzer's works are more ambiguous than her statements suggest. Everything is placed side by side, without comment or context. What is ironic and what is sincere? I would argue that a text like Solanas's *SCUM Manifesto* clearly covers both sides — simultaneously "scary" and "deeply felt." There are many lines that blur and overlap, which is the reason manifestos make such compelling yet uncomfortable reading. Even stripped of their particular contexts, Holzer's inflammatory texts retain their power as manifestos, because they retain their passion and (mad) dedication. Manifestos have to *mean* it. This is also what gets them into trouble — when they mean it so much that, frustrated by the limitations of polite language, they reach beyond measured words to make their target *feel* their point—to make it *hurt*. Solanas certainly knew this. Marinetti, who lectured passionately on "The Necessity and Beauty of Violence" before the war, knew it too. As the narrator in Joanna Walsh's digital age novel *Break.up* (2018) says: "Love and writing are so close: both involve a little violence."

37. Provocation

The opening lines of famous manifestos suggest that provocation is the goal from the start. Futurist manifestos usually begin with scenes of violent action or insults aimed directly at their audience. In his "Lecture to the English on Futurism" (1910), Marinetti warns: "I'll tell you straight away what we think of you." He adds that "every good Futurist should be discourteous twenty times a day." This is a clever approach because nothing is more fascinating than having all of our features, good and bad, described to us in careful and frank detail by someone we've never met. Trotsky, Breton and Rivera began their manifesto *Towards a Free Revolutionary Art*: "We can say without exaggeration that never has civilization been menaced so seriously as today." This kind of opener grabs you by the collar. It establishes who is in charge—which in the manifesto's case is always (at least performatively) the author. The *Dada Cannibalistic Manifesto* (1920) begins with the command: "You are all accused; stand up." Sometimes the intention to shock is obvious, like the long opening sentence of the *SCUM Manifesto*, which ends with a call to "overthrow the government, eliminate the money system, institute complete automation and destroy the male sex." Other times, as in the case of Gilbert and George, it provokes with its unexpected civility: "Always be smartly dressed, well groomed relaxed and friendly polite and in complete control."

38. Anger

John Sinclair, the Detroit-based poet, Yippie, manager of the band MC5, and co-founder of the White Panther Party (a far-left, anti-racist white counterpart to the Black Panthers), issued the following manifesto in 1968 on behalf of the White Panthers' Ministry of Information:

> Our program is cultural revolution through a total assault on the culture... We take our program with us everywhere we go and use any means necessary to expose people to it. Our culture, our art, the music, newspapers, books, posters, our clothing, our homes, the way we walk and talk, the way our hair grows, the way we smoke dope and fuck and eat and sleep—it is all one message, and the message is FREEDOM... BE FREE, goddammit, and fuck all them old dudes.

The Hate Socialist Collective, writing in a 2009 special issue of *Poetry* magazine to celebrate the centenary of *The Founding and Manifesto of Futurism*, declared:

> like you, oh *Poetry*, we propose to reanimate the manifesto. We will first require the following things: a century of revolutions. Delight and terror. Shit on the curatorial. Shit on bankers and trusts. Shit on ourselves...Those who make a manifesto by halves dig their own graves.

Marinetti's call for "violence" as an essential ingredient of the manifesto has survived through generations of manifesto writing. In the 1960s and 1970s numerous urban guerrilla groups, including the Red Army Faction/Baader-Meinhof group in Germany, the Red Brigades in Italy, the Angry Brigade in Britain and the Weather Underground in the US, waged war on what they saw as state violence through a campaign of shootings and bombings, often accompanied by a steady stream of manifestos or communiqués. *Communiqué 1* (1970) by the Angry Brigade claims responsibility for violent actions, lists targets and reads a bit like a poem:

Fascism & oppression
will be smashed
Embassies (Spanish Embassy machine gunned Thursday)
High Pigs
Spectacles
Judges
Property

"Anger is an energy," as that latter-day Dadaist Johnny Rotten said. (If you haven't read *Lipstick Traces*, Greil Marcus's "secret history" of the roots of punk in the European avant-garde, I recommend it.) Even more than punk, however, it is hip-hop that captures the true spirit of the avant-garde manifesto: proud, arrogant, boastful, profane, combative, brawling, technologically cutting edge, rhetorically aggressive, frequently masculinist and unbothered by accusations of plagiarism. Rap music and its offshoots put provocation and principles into every track: from Gang Starr's "Manifest" to Wu-Tang Clan's "Fast Shadow" ("What I'm manifestin' each day is a lesson") to grime artist Stormzy's blistering freestyle rap at the 2018 Brit Awards in which he called out Prime Minister Theresa May for her government's failures. Punk has the anger, nihilism and arrogance, but it lacks the rhetorical flourish, the formalized rules of engagement, the sense of competition and the use of technology. Demonstrating just how common anger is in manifestos, the artist R. B. Kitaj actually *apologizes* (in the *First Diasporist Manifesto*) for not being angry enough. He knows the rules of the genre, and knows that he is failing to live up to them. "I haven't read Breton or Lewis or Marinetti since I was eighteen," he explains. Many of the fiercest manifestos succeed because they aren't afraid to tap into emotion, including aggression, which is a source of vitality too often tamped down in the name of reason. We are said to be living in an "Age of Rage" — often righteous and revolutionary, but equally reactionary. The zeitgeist is reflected in the titles of recent bestsellers: *Fire and Fury, Fear, Age of Anger, Good and Mad, Rage Becomes Her*. Monikers such as "Digital Age" and "Information Age" suddenly seem inadequate: too bland to describe the current climate; too tame to capture the reality of the age we're living through, when everything is a fight.

39. Screaming to be heard

The anger and frustration that came through in manifestos of the first-wave avant-garde was not merely an attention-seeking pose. It was a reaction to the carnage of the First World War, a howl of outrage against the "civilization" that failed so badly in 1914 (and would continue to do so, over and over, throughout the twentieth century). This was true particularly of Dada, but other groups gave expression to their outrage with various forms of primitivism (especially in the childish sense) or nihilism. One short-lived movement formed in 1919 in Cologne, Germany simply called itself "Stupid." The young men and women that started such movements were, of course, drawn from the same generation that died in vast numbers on the front lines during the war. Their performance of childish anger, like that of the counterculture of the 1960s, was in part an expression of desperate powerlessness and frustration at the obstinacy of the paternal nation state. The manifesto, of course, is fundamentally *not* an essay. This is a key point of difference: that the revolutionary manifesto is ruled by the heart, not the head. As Avital Ronell wrote in her introduction to the 2004 edition of the *SCUM Manifesto*: "Sometimes you have to scream to be heard."

40. Making threats

The temptation to go beyond rhetoric is always present in the manifesto. The impulse to write a manifesto often comes out of an extreme frustration with the status quo, so the idea that a page of demands and principles will not go far enough—that direct action is needed—is understandable. In his diary Derek Jarman expresses this sense of frustration in the context of the HIV/AIDS crisis of the 1980s and the inaction of the British government under Margaret Thatcher. "We need Burroughs' gay soldiers. As I write, only the niceties and constraints of an English upbringing stop me reaching for a gun." There is a dark side to all this rhetorical violence, of course, seen especially in the issuing of manifestos in recent years by mass murderers driven by a lethal combination of delusional narcissism and hate-filled ideology. The pre-war avant-garde in Europe was notoriously aggressive and full of threats—as if, like many politicians at the time, they were itching for the all-out war they soon got. In an essay published in *The Egoist* in February 1914, Ezra Pound wrote: "The artist has at last been aroused to the fact that the war between him and the world is a war without truce. That his only remedy is slaughter." The artistic avant-garde now seemed firmly tied up in the kind of violent battle being staged by revolutionary political groups like the Suffragettes, whom Marinetti accompanied on a window-smashing campaign during one of his visits to London. At the same time, looking back on the pre-war period 2 decades later, having endured the actual war that followed, Wyndham Lewis doubted whether the threat Vorticism and Futurism posed to society was taken seriously by the public or only consumed as entertainment: "it was acclaimed the best joke ever...they felt as safe as houses. So did I."

41. The kill in killjoy

Feminist manifestos—or any challenge to any system of oppression, whether patriarchal, colonial or otherwise—are often seen as violent provocations, no matter how rhetorical the threat they pose. Sara Ahmed makes this point in *A Killjoy Manifesto* (2017), reminding us to "remember the *kill* in killjoy." She writes: "feminism is often described as a form of murder; calling for the end of the system that makes 'men' is often understood as killing men." Ahmed evokes the figure of Valerie Solanas and the convenient fantasy of the "murderous feminist." Solanas's rage drove her to fill the *SCUM Manifesto* with rhetorical violence, including some very visceral threats: "If SCUM ever marches, it will be over the President's stupid, sickening face; if SCUM ever strikes, it will be in the dark with a six-inch blade." Solanas notoriously crossed the line into actual violence by shooting Andy Warhol on June 3, 1968. Tired of feminism's retreat into polite and unthreatening forms of protest, Jessa Crispin declares in *Why I Am Not a Feminist: A Feminist Manifesto* (2018): "I am angry. And I do pose a threat." Such insistence on the potential for real revolutionary violence behind the manifesto's fiery rhetoric has a long history. In *The Communist Manifesto*, for example, Marx and Engels quip, with eyebrows archly raised: "you reproach us with intending to do away with your property. Precisely so; this is just what we intend." Long before they were used to threaten the powers that be with imminent revolution, manifestos were used to declare war on enemy states. In this usage, a "war manifesto" is defined as "a (1) public document (2) issued by a sovereign (3) against another sovereign (4) containing the reasons for going to war." You can hear echoes of this history not only in the threats of actual violence but also in the cries of warring factions of the avant-garde throughout the last century. "Read my manifesto and it will tell you what I am," Solanas told reporters outside the 13th Precinct in New York. Manifestos are always, often literally, at the bleeding edge of culture and politics. The threats they contain are potent because they are sincere: there is always enough instability, enough wildness about the manifesto to give it real menace—the possibility, near or distant, of real danger, real action, actual revolution.

42. Disruption

Manifestos tend to follow the motto "move fast and break things." Futurism is a dramatic case in point: burn the libraries, flood the museums, abolish pasta. "When the world feels stuck, the manifesto—like the work of art—is a mode to disrupt it," as Daniel Rourke, co-author with Morehshin Allahyari of *The 3D Additivist Manifesto* (2015), told me regarding their choice of medium. Of course, there are important differences between true social and artistic disruption, on one hand, and the disruption of platform capitalism. The former, seen for example in grassroots online social movements like #MeToo, seeks to disrupt and overturn a corrupt and toxic status quo that has existed, unchallenged, for far too long. It is a mistake to allow the latter to get away with co-opting markers of truly radical change. Big tech companies plunder the vocabulary of radicalism, using it to describe exploitative business practices that use legal loopholes to get around decent working conditions and other hard won basic human rights. That isn't the revolution you're looking for.

43. Bodies matter

On February 8, 1996, John Perry Barlow published his landmark manifesto *A Declaration of the Independence of Cyberspace*. In the short text Barlow shunned the hoary old world of "flesh and steel" for the brave new one of pure disembodied "Mind." He declared (in what can only be imagined as a booming voice): "I come from Cyberspace, the new home of Mind." In fact, Barlow was not writing from cyberspace at all; the manifesto was written in a hotel room in Davos, Switzerland, during the annual meeting of the World Economic Forum. Its other signs of naiveté aside, one particular blind spot of the manifesto seems blindingly obvious: bodies *always* matter. We can never entirely escape our embodied realities, just as we can't easily escape our economic ones. And while manifestos might sometimes pose as abstract universal truths — principles far removed from situated realities and the concerns of everyday life — they invoke bodily metaphors with a frequency that belies any claim to ethereal transcendence. Bodies *matter*. Manifestos are material, even when they are digital.

44. Bodies in action

Manifestos rely more than a little on bodily metaphors. Whistler often spoke of "slaying" or "scalping" his critics. Dada manifestos overflow with excrement. When Marina Abramović read her manifesto *An Artist's Life* at the Serpentine Gallery's Manifesto Marathon in 2008, she was joined by a chorus of men and women dressed in white (for sperm) and red (for menstrual blood). Why? Because bodily metaphors are vivid and compelling: Nietzschean images of flesh and blood are more striking than Kantian philosophical abstractions. More than that, manifestos are anti-reason, anti-intellect—they not only include the body, they often *privilege* body over mind. VNS Matrix's *Cyberfeminist Manifesto for the 21st Century* (1991) declares:

> We are the modern cunt
> positive anti reason
> unbounded unleashed unforgiving
> we see art with our cunt we make art with our cunt

The *White Panther Manifesto* (1968) made liberation an explicitly bodily act, expressed in bodily terms: "We breathe revolution... We will do anything we can to drive people crazy out of their heads and into their bodies." Janet Lyon has argued that manifestos represent "bodies in struggle rather than simply ideas in contention." She makes the interesting point that the Suffragettes, who were militant in bodily terms, "incit[ing] physical rebellion," putting their bodies on the line and risking death through direct action, stood in stark contrast to the Vorticists, their contemporaries in the art world, whose "militant discourse...was confined mostly to the page." In *Wanderlust* Rebecca Solnit describes walking as resistance, a political act, literally making manifest, taking up public space. In *A Killjoy Manifesto*, Sara Ahmed writes: "our bodies become our tools." Most or all of the points in Chimamanda Ngozi Adichie's *Dear Ijeawele, or, A Feminist Manifesto in Fifteen Suggestions* (2017) relate explicitly to the body, in subject or metaphor or both. For example, the fourth suggestion warns of "Feminism Lite": "Being a feminist is like being pregnant. You either are or you are not." Of course, bodies are the terrain on which many battles for equality are fought. The manifesto of the radical 1930s West Indian magazine *Légitime Défense* declares: "We rise up here against all those who are not suffocated by this capitalist, Christian, bourgeois world to which, involuntarily, our protesting bodies belong."

45. The new spirit

Apollinaire was one of the great manifesto writers: bold, brash and endlessly inventive. He was the kind of radical writer who gets picked up when the *Mona Lisa* goes missing from the Louvre. (This actually happened in 1911. He suggested the authorities question his friend Pablo Picasso, which they did, though neither was the thief.) Apollinaire brought the Marquis de Sade back from obscurity, and coined the term Surrealism. His last manifesto, *The New Spirit and the Poets*, was published shortly before his death in 1918. Apollinaire had suffered a shrapnel wound to the head in 1916 and was trepanned for a cure; he was never quite the same, and died of influenza 2 days before the armistice. His manifesto's famous *rappel à l'ordre* — the "call to order" — a return to Classicism and turning away from Romanticism after the carnage and chaos of the First World War, is an example of the manifesto's tendency to draw a line in history — a line against the past. No more looking backward, no more dwelling in the past, no more tragedy and defeat, only youth and optimism, hope in the present and future, in art and society alike: "The new spirit which will dominate the poetry of the entire world...."

46. Dramatic rupture

The impulse to draw a line against the past and look toward the future, to make a clean break, is an impulse that is ripe for metaphor: the wind of change, the new dawn, the toppled statue, the cleansing fire. Zero, an art movement born in the ruins of postwar Germany, declared with performative hopefulness: "Zero is stillness. Zero is the beginning." The desire for radical disruption or *tabula rasa* has been expressed in countless metaphors by manifesto writers. In *The Communist Manifesto* Marx and Engels describe the dramatic shift to modernity under capitalism as a kind of magical sublimation: "All that is solid melts into air." To the Vorticists, the Victorian era is a vampire that is still sucking the life out of modern London. In *Slap in the Face of Public Taste* (1912), the Hylaea group of Russian Futurists memorably describe the desire to break with the past as physically tossing away the previous generation: "Throw Pushkin, Dostoevsky, Tolstoy, etc., etc. overboard from the Ship of Modernity." The Italian Futurists express their urge to break with the past in destructive terms: "Take up your pickaxes, your axes and hammers, and wreck, wreck the venerable cities!" Only when the past has been destroyed will young artists be free of its suffocating grasp. Every manifesto in effect declares: Rip it up and start again.

47. Intolerable and untenable

What the manifesto marks above all is a summing up and a decisive turning away from how things are now. In the manifesto things are always intolerable and untenable: a new path is still possible, but it requires a dramatic change of direction. One slightly trivial example which nonetheless illustrates the subversive and antagonistic attitude toward authority expressed in many manifestos is the artist David Hockney's *Manifesto for Smoking* (2008), written shortly after a smoking ban went into effect across the UK. Hockney was apparently upset on principle, given that he had lived in California since 1964 and smoking had already been banned in that state for 2 decades. He railed against "a small fanatical group in Brussels" trying to control laws in Britain, and ended his rant: "Stand up against the dreary conformity that is spreading much too fast. DEATH AWAITS YOU EVEN IF YOU DO NOT SMOKE." Another example is a manifesto Derek Jarman wrote in his Slade School notebooks, dated "Winter 1964" (when he was 22) and subtitled "Tentative ideas for a manifesto after 1 1/3 years at an art school." Jarman first describes the state of things: "It is evident that the arts have been ossified into respective spheres unnaturally, dancing, the opera house, the theatre, architecture, the concert hall, etc." With all the fervor of youth he then declares in unequivocal tones — despite the "tentative" in the title — what must be done to fight this fragmentation and ossification in the arts. A complete structural overhaul is needed. Roles must be reversed. "The audience must become participators, the creators. The artist must abrogate his mystery." With the shift away from the past toward the future often comes a new optimism, but sometimes that optimistic future is shaky and uncertain. In "My Fascism (A Few Truths)," from a book of manifestos and essays by the Russian socialist poet Kirill Medvedev called *It's No Good* (2012),

Medvedev states: "The political and cultural situation in Russia makes me fear for the future." He admits that in the chaos of the present there is, maybe, "a chance to start from scratch." But unlike Marinetti he does not want to "predict anything terrible happening" — another violent revolution. Instead, he says, "I'll just say what I hope for: I hope someday to live in my homeland, with my son Bogdan, and to practice my art, unpoliticized, as an ordinary private citizen." That is not how things are in the present, it remains a dream of hope set sometime in the future. Auden's line again comes to mind: "But to-day the struggle."

48. Anti-

Almost immediately as you read the opening rules of the *Dada Manifesto* of 1918, it becomes obvious that none of those rules can be taken at face value. Tzara declares: "I am neither for nor against and I don't explain because I hate common sense." And: "I am writing a manifesto and there is nothing I want." Hmm, that's rather suspicious behavior for a manifesto. The Imagist manifesto of 1913, signed by F. S. Flint but penned by Ezra Pound, offers the incongruous statement: "They had not published a manifesto." Yes, but. The Turkish *D Group Manifesto* (1933) states: "This is not new painting...I am not expounding a theory." What links together all these manifestos that doth protest too much? They are examples of a sub-category I call the "anti-manifesto" — the manifesto that appears to undermine, negate or contradict its own purpose. They're fairly common — not least because irony, parody, negation and other features of the anti-manifesto are more rule than exception among avant-garde manifestos generally. What anti-manifestos do is say something, even something serious, while claiming to say nothing, or nothing serious. The anti-manifesto might be a parody of serious manifestos, whether revolutionary or party political; but it is also a reaction against the sort of avant-garde manifesto that follows the template laid down by Futurism. These anti-manifestos seek, with good reason, to deflate Futurism's bombastic rhetoric, its belief in technological progress, uncritical faith in the new, and military triumphalism. Anti-manifestos undercut their own purpose in the midst of their performance, but their serious intent, even if purely critical or reactionary, remains intact. Anti-manifestos refuse to do what manifestos seemingly exist to do: to preach, to convince and convert. The philosopher Timothy Morton's *Being Ecological* (2018), which could reasonably be called a manifesto for ecological thinking, opens with several instances of anti-manifesto tactics: "Rest assured this book is not going to preach at you. It also contains no ecological facts, no shocking revelations about our world, no ethical or political advice, and no grand tour of ecological thinking. This is a pretty useless ecology book, actually." Writers of anti-manifestos test the boundaries to see where they exist, reverse or push back against expected logic, or try to undo or unsettle generic constraints in other ways. These and other manifestos like them refuse to admit, against clear evidence to the contrary, that they are manifestos at all. Manifestos are often criticized for being too blunt. But the best avant-garde examples, including many "anti-manifestos," cleverly foreground their own rhetorical features, displaying the self-critical tendency that Marx refers to in *The Eighteenth Brumaire of Louis Bonaparte* (1852). In fact the anti-manifesto is useful today precisely for its modeling of a critical response to technology-as-religion and capitalist boosterism. The way in which anti-manifestos of the past century deployed irony and critical distance to resist Futurism's uncritical embrace of technology, nationalism and war is an important lesson for our times. Anti-manifestos represent a form of critical writing that should not be overlooked.

49. Seeds

Summing up the battle of isms in his essay "Manifesto = Theatre," Martin Puchner wrote: "No movement, it seems, can do without a manifesto; the result is a veritable manifesto-war that leads to ever-more extreme proclamations and attention-mongering rhetoric." Owing to this situation of intense competition, there has been a lot of violence in the first half of this book—sorry! And there is more to come. The manifesto is a bombastic and aggressive genre. That said, however, there are gentler and subtler ways to write manifestos that are also effective and still in their way provocative. While drastic times do sometimes call for drastic action, not every manifesto has to tear down walls, burn libraries, flood museums or kill all men. Lately I've been thinking about a manifesto written by MIT Media Lab director Joichi Ito called *Resisting Reduction* (2017). Ito uses the manifesto as a "seed essay" for starting discussions and gathering commentary (which highlights the collaborative potential of online manifesto writing). New iterations of Ito's manifesto will incorporate the feedback collected online. Collaborative writing and transparency are two of the manifesto's best features, as is the use of provocation, gentle in this case, to generate new ideas. With its rich history of manifesto writing, Europe still produces a lot of socially engaged and often government funded plans for change. A manifesto written in 2009 by the Polish Committee for Radical Change in Culture (later published in English by the Freee Art Collective) is one example that pushes back against the privatization of culture and calls for recognition of the important role the arts play in a free and democratic society. Its demands include increased public education about contemporary art as well as the "elimination of the centralized, bureaucratic model of governing culture" in favor of local councils. Another example is *A People's Manifesto for Wildlife* (2018), launched in the UK by the English naturalist Chris

Packham with the help of Robert Macfarlane and others. Written with substantial contributions from leading academics and government ministers, the manifesto is political but non-partisan, "written to be accessible to everyone" (it also comes in a longer, fully referenced version), and "deliberately incomplete" so as to encourage contributions from the public. Increasingly, academics and curators are seeking not only to study social, political, artistic and environmental movements from the outside, but also to work with and from within these movements. Manifestos, in contrast to traditional academic papers or monographs with their strict format and limited reach, serve this purpose. (There are endless examples, including Rosa Menkman's gloriously glitchy *Glitch Studies Manifesto*, Robert Pepperell's *Posthuman Manifesto* and Cary Nelson's still relevant *Manifesto of a Tenured Radical*.) The manifesto may be viewed as a gathering point or intersection to promote positive collective action and resistance, prying open discursive and imaginative spaces and forcing new ideas into the public view. As Garnet Hertz states in his five-point manifesto for the zine-like pamphlet *Disobedient Electronics: Protest* (2016): "If we are living in a post-truth time, we should focus on trying to make progressive arguments and facts more legible and engaging to a wide and diverse audience." In their argument for platform cooperativism, scholar-activists Trebor Scholz and Nathan Schneider posit that the source of platform capitalism's power is the culture or ecosystem built up by its corporations: "the festivals, the meetups, the memes, the manifestos—that share norms for what kinds of practices are expected and celebrated." Redefining and changing norms requires the cultivation of an alternative discursive ecosystem to that of platform capitalism, which includes writing new manifestos. Promoting cooperativism and constructive change—these are some noble aims you should keep in mind. There are other times, of course, when you realize you'll need to burn it all right down to the ground and start again from scratch.

Failures

50. A will of one's own

"[M]ore and more I come to loathe any domination of one over another; any leadership, any imposition of the will." Virginia Woolf wrote these words in her diary on March 19, 1919, long before the "political" manifestos that established her place in feminist theory. Her sentiment here captures the central conflict of all revolutionary manifestos: there is, on one hand, the seed of discontent that brings about the need to write; on the other lies the act of writing, which often involves the risk of imposing your will upon others. Woolf's sensitivity to this conflict within the manifesto may be one reason why the Bloomsbury Group of which she was a central figure never produced anything like a collective statement. Two texts by Woolf to which the manifesto label is frequently, if loosely, applied are *Mr Bennett and Mrs Brown* (1923) and *Modern Fiction* (1925). In these and other essays of the period, Woolf can be seen working out fundamental aesthetic principles of modernism—how we perceive, and how writers should best represent, the interior and exterior world.

51. Set fire to the old hypocrisies

Woolf's later manifestos, however, including *A Room of One's Own* (1929) and *Three Guineas* (1938), mark a striking shift. She becomes politically engaged while managing to avoid the "imposition of the will" she so disliked in others—and which she had depicted so powerfully in the fate of the shell-shocked young veteran Septimus Warren Smith at the hands of the medical establishment in her novel *Mrs Dalloway* (1925). Woolf invents a new kind of manifesto, an alternative to the masculinist model established by Marinetti. Especially in *Three Guineas*, a radical indictment of patriarchal society and the continuing exclusion of women, she seems to offer a direct reply to this model, even producing some incendiary rhetoric of her own ("Take this guinea and with it burn the college to the ground. Set fire to the old hypocrisies"). At one point she is asked by an unnamed man, "How in your opinion are we to prevent war?" and she must confront "a precipice" of inequality, "a gulf so deeply cut between us that for three years and more I have been sitting on my side of it wondering whether it is any use to try to speak across it." Ironically, she is asked to sign a manifesto. Woolf laments: "We have no weapon with which to enforce our will." She must shout to be heard above the braying male voices, even as she attempts to deconstruct and rewrite the terms of expression and debate. The dictator is found, Woolf declares, in the guise of the male chauvinist, not only in Italy or Germany but "here among us, raising his ugly head, spitting his poison... in the heart of England." "And is not the woman who has to breathe that poison and to fight that insect," she asks, "fighting the Fascist or the Nazi as surely as those who fight him with arms?" Fascism begins at home. The violent imposition of the will is everywhere, and everywhere its perpetrators must be unmasked.

52. Beyond the masculinist model

Rather than give in to destructive rage, however, Woolf sets it up as only one of several possible reactions to the challenges and barriers faced by women in Britain. Her approach is defined by its broad, multi-vocal style, and by the composure of the editor who controls the different voices. One voice, for example, in the second part of the essay, lists concrete examples of what could be done if women were allowed into the professions to earn equal pay with men:

> You could finance a woman's party in the House of Commons. You could run a daily newspaper committed to a conspiracy, not of silence, but of speech. You could get pensions for spinsters; those victims of the patriarchal system, whose allowance is insufficient and whose board and lodging are no longer thrown in. You could get equal pay for equal work. You could provide every mother with chloroform when her child is born; bring down the maternal death-rate from four in every thousand to none at all, perhaps.

For all its anger and practical energy, *Three Guineas* is more a utopian meditation than an avant-garde manifesto in the Marinettian sense. But this should not be viewed as a shortcoming: in many ways the avant-garde manifesto represented precisely the aggressive and paternalistic "mansplaining" tendencies that Woolf was fighting against. With *Three Guineas* Woolf launched a powerful critique of the manifesto that rose to prominence during the early twentieth century. Rather than try to be "one of the boys," Woolf resists the temptation to write propaganda of any sort, and chooses instead to put her energy into, as she put it: "finding new words and creating new methods."

53. Performance anxiety (this is my gun)

In Marinetti's model, the manifesto's strength—the Nietzschean force of will that Woolf finds so distasteful—is also its greatest weakness. The manifesto's "hysteria" is a masculine one, an overcompensation, a performance anxiety that is assuaged through the unleashing of violence. As suggested above, the avant-garde manifesto after Marinetti modeled itself in part on "war manifestos" of the past. Futurism in particular exhibited a proto-fascistic desire for domination and exploitation, a mindset masked as or mistaken for bold adventure—like the old settler's cry of "manifest destiny," the supposed God-given right and duty to conquer and colonize foreign lands. Applied to art this meant destroying everything in its path in order to rebuild from a clean slate. As one Futurist theater manifesto from 1915 declares: "ABOLISH THE FARCE, THE VAUDEVILLE, THE SKETCH, THE COMEDY, THE SERIOUS DRAMA, AND TRAGEDY, AND CREATE IN THEIR PLACE THE MANY FORMS OF FUTURIST THEATER." But why in all caps? Why the need to shout? In the *SCUM Manifesto*, Solanas describes male violence as stemming from a deep-seated sense of inadequacy:

> The male is eaten up with tension…eaten up with hate—not rational hate that is directed at those who abuse or insult you—but irrational, indiscriminate hate…hatred, at bottom, of his own worthless self.
>
> Gratuitous violence, besides "proving" he's a "Man," serves as an outlet for his hate and, in addition…provides him with a little sexual thrill.

There is a famous scene in Stanley Kubrick's Vietnam War film *Full Metal Jacket* (1987) that perfectly evokes the type of violent and phallocentric manifesto pioneered by Marinetti. It is the scene in which new Marine Corps recruits in boot camp learn that a "rifle" should never be confused with a "gun." The young soldiers parade through the barracks in their underwear, accompanied by their drill sergeant, grabbing their genitals and hollering: *"This is my rifle, this is my gun. This one's for fighting, this one's for fun."* It might be meant as humorous, and it does look ludicrous, but for many viewers the scene is surely terrifying in its implications. The Futurists seem often to have confused their rifles with their guns—which was for fighting again? And which for fun? In their desire to fight in the coming European war, in their haste to prove their virility and masculinity as artists, the young male Futurists confused their genitalia not only with rifles, but with paintbrushes and pens as well.

54. Screeching to be heard

Judith Butler argues that the performative is always melancholic, since the performer knows the role is only a fantasy. Both the compensatory violence and the melancholy seem right enough in the case of Marinetti; but it is Martin Puchner who sums it up best in an essay called "Screeching Voices: Avant-Garde Manifestos in the Cabaret" (2000). Puchner argues that the avant-garde manifesto, from Italian Futurism to Dada performances in the Cabaret Voltaire, "compensates for [its] lack of authority... through the demonstrative over-confidence and aggressiveness that will remain the marks of the genre" (hence "screeching voices"). I can't help but think of Basil Fawlty, the snobbish and tyrannical but ultimately powerless hotel manager played by John Cleese in the BBC series *Fawlty Towers*, screeching in vain at poor Manuel, the waiter from Barcelona, as he tries, and always fails, to assert his will and authority through sheer force of volume. On the other hand, the screeching also mimics the amplified, hyped up sound and appearance of modernity: the advertising copy and eye-catching tricks, and the screeching British tabloid headlines so deftly adopted by *BLAST* in 1914.

55. Sheer macho absurdity

And yet there is humor too. The Futurist theater manifesto quoted above suggests a kind of knowing laughter in the face of the sheer macho absurdity of the enterprise. (If it is not clear in the example of theater, try keeping a straight face while reading the *Manifesto of Futurist Cuisine* with its injunction to abolish pasta.) "Anti-manifestos" suggest defensive maneuvers in anticipation of the ultimately ineffectual nature of artistic protest in times of real crisis. Tristan Tzara, sounding more like Groucho than Karl Marx, wrote in his *Dada Manifesto* of 1918: "I am on principle against manifestos, as I am also against principles." The Vorticists conceded that behind all their blasting and bravado lay something much more tenuous, propped up by the support (financial and otherwise) of women: "a couple of women and one or two not very reliable men," as Lewis later wrote. And despite all their wild hyperbolic claims, the Futurists predicted in their very first manifesto that Futurism would be short-lived (shorter lived than it actually was, in fact)—that before long "younger and stronger men will probably throw us in the wastebasket like useless manuscripts," adding masochistically: "we want it to happen!" This ironic self-awareness is ultimately what distinguishes manifestos like those of Futurism, which do endorse violent and misogynistic ideas, from the much graver rhetoric and promises of actual violence laid out in recent manifestos by white supremacists and "incel" groups, which are bereft of those redeeming qualities.

56. Violence

Margaret Atwood once said that while men worry that women will laugh at them, women fear men will kill them. Manifestos may be full of hope, bright futures and noble principles—but violence is also baked into their DNA. The first Futurist manifesto states that art "can be nothing but violence, cruelty, and injustice." Walter Benjamin wrote in his essay "The Work of Art in the Age of Mechanical Reproduction" about the way Futurism and Fascism aestheticize violence, and this is nowhere more evident than in the Futurist manifestos. The 1960s were full of armed liberation struggles that paired images of revolutionaries with guns and slogans—"By Any Means Necessary" or "We're looking for people who like to *draw*." Art doesn't have to be comfortable; it is often better when it's uncomfortable. But you have to ask what purpose the violence serves. The essential dichotomy in all revolutionary manifestos lies between the desire to transgress and the will to authority. As the Norwegian mass murderer Anders Breivik demonstrated in *2083: A European Declaration of Independence*, a rambling 1500-page collage of racist and misogynistic propaganda, the internet provides endless content for manifestos promoting hatred and violence. One of the numerous sources copied into Breivik's diatribe, along with passages from George Orwell and Thomas Jefferson, is Ted Kaczinski's *Industrial Society and Its Future*, the "Unabomber Manifesto." Disseminating the manifesto was Kaczinski's final demand; Breivik's manifesto begins with meticulous instructions for translating and spreading it across the internet via social media and torrent sites. (Long before the Unabomber, the *Front de Libération du Québec* made Canadian history by having their manifesto for an independent Quebec read in full on state television in October 1970 as a ransom demand for the release of kidnapped British Trade Commissioner

James Cross.) The issue of "wounded" or "failed" masculinity and manifesto violence has resurfaced recently in the media coverage of terrorist attacks by so-called "incels" — "involuntary celibates" — starting with the 2014 Isla Vista shootings by Elliot Rodger and his widely distributed manifesto *My Twisted World*. In Cory Doctorow's first novel, *Down and Out in the Magic Kingdom* (2003), death has been cured and recreational assassination is the norm, so you can kill someone just to make a point, as a kind of rhetorical flourish. This seems like a suitable analogy for "bad" manifestos and their fantasy of stepping beyond the limitations of language — beyond rhetorical into actual violence. It's a strange fantasy, isn't it? But it speaks to a desire to bridge the virtual and actual, which has a new poignancy in the internet age, where there exists a split between social media use that brings people together around a common cause, and social media use that increases social isolation to the point of profound alienation and anti-social violence. It is difficult at this point not to think of President Trump's chillingly despotic words to Bob Woodward: "Real power is fear."

57. Destroy the male sex

Violent manifesto rhetoric isn't limited to fascists and misogynists. Valentine de Saint-Point's *Manifesto of Futurist Woman*, a response to Marinetti's "contempt," declares: "Let woman find once more her cruelty and her violence." Valerie Solanas is a direct descendent. The *SCUM Manifesto* has perhaps the best opening line of any manifesto in the twentieth century, exemplifying what is at once most thrilling and most disturbing about the genre:

> Life in this society being, at best, an utter bore and no aspect of society being at all relevant to women, there remains to civic-minded, responsible, thrill-seeking females only to overthrow the government, eliminate the money system, institute complete automation and destroy the male sex.

Manifestos give a powerful voice to those who feel powerless, frustrated or aggrieved for whatever reason—justified or not. So it might be Jessa Crispin saying: "My feminism… is a cleansing fire." Or Sara Ahmed: "you have to let the violence spill, all over the pages." But this powerful voice might also be used by someone like Elliot Rodger, who posted a video statement on YouTube and sent out his 100,000-word manifesto giving his defense of patriarchal domination and sexual entitlement in the midst of his killing spree in Isla Vista, California, in 2014. Or Dylann Roof, who uploaded a violent racist diatribe before massacring nine black parishioners in a church in Charleston, South Carolina, in 2016. (The manifesto ends with the morbid line: "Please forgive any typos, I didnt have time to check it.") What should we make of the manifesto's violent past—a past that haunts and shapes it still?

58. On cruelty

Maybe it's the mask that invites cruelty to the manifesto: nothing personal; or, the delirium of the mask. *Did I say that?* Or maybe it comes from being born in the modernist era—all that masculine "hardness" and cold, detached, machine-like, anti-romantic abstraction promoted by Wyndham Lewis, Ezra Pound and T. E. Hulme—drawing on European philosophers from around the turn of the century like Nietzsche, Sorel (*Reflections on Violence*), Worringer (*Abstraction and Empathy*)and Stirner (*The Ego and Its Own*). Perhaps it was the imminent threat and then the traumatic experience of mechanized warfare; young men (and women) steeling themselves for the carnage that would dominate the first half of the twentieth century. "To be severe and cruel," as Tristan Tzara wrote in 1919. There is a danger with manifestos of looking at the world as having no friends, only enemies, like America under the Trump Doctrine—of seeing only isms and schisms. As I mentioned earlier, manifestos, like Silicon Valley tech companies, tend to operate on the motto "move fast and break things." This can be thrilling and innovative, or it can simply be reckless and authoritarian. The French sociologist Bruno Latour has written about Silicon Valley's destructively "heroic, Promethean, hubristic dream of action": "Go forward, break radically with the past and the consequences will take care of themselves!" The basic cruelty that is present in many manifestos, whatever the origin of that cruelty, may be a source of strength (bold, blunt, big picture)—but it also must be viewed as a kind of failure. The desire for rebirth, *tabula rasa*, the razing of the past to pave the way for the imagined future—the "break a few eggs" approach—can have real consequences, as the manifestos claiming to justify mass killings in this century prove. By rhetorical habit manifestos are radical and extreme, never modest or incremental, which leads in some cases to catastrophic errors of judgment. The tendency toward cruelty has been boldly countered by a few writers and artists over the decades, including Frank O'Hara in his *Personism* manifesto—which mocks, from a humane and worldly perspective, the uptight modernism he knew so well. Tzara's nihilism aside, many Dada manifestos also countered the explicit cruelty of Futurism with warmth and absurd humor. In recent years the British artist David Shrigley has lampooned the failure of manifestos and other grand schemes to fix the world's problems in books with titles like *Weak Messages Create Bad Situations: A Manifesto* (2014) and *Coherent Plan for a New and Better Society* (2018). Shrigley counters the ignorance and disastrous stupidity that are rife in contemporary politics with subtle, and sometimes not so subtle, humor. The cover of *Weak Messages* features a characteristically simple drawing: a hammer labeled "the message" and a nail labeled "the recipient of the message." When you read a lot of manifestos all at once you sometimes start to feel like the nail.

59. Extremes

I've mentioned the phrase "isms and schisms" a few times now. The original source is Malcolm Bradbury and James McFarlane's *Modernism: 1890-1930* (1976):

> As in all sects, religious or political—and it was on such analogues that the movements [of modernism] formed and acted—"ism" tended toward schism, denominationalism. So they appropriately rallied followers, mounted displays, enacted themselves in public. Hence of considerable importance to their history are the manifestos they presented...

We can agree by this time—I hope!—that manifestos are important. But what about the tendency toward factionalism and antipathy that manifestos seem to encourage? The division of the populace into two camps, us versus them, pro- versus anti-, insiders versus outsiders, red versus blue, is increasingly a problem of our times. Social media effects such as amplification, dehumanization of the other, and sorting into algorithmic echo chambers serve to feed this problem. Polarization is a seductive and often effective strategy employed by manifesto writers to win converts. It is a powerfully romantic notion, as the Russian Futurists recognized: "To stand on a rock of the word 'we' amidst the sea of boos and outrage." Politics today is becoming rapidly more polarized and partisan, with tribal allegiances taking the place of objective facts (crowd size, on-the-record comments). It might even be conceded, on the topic of failures— with great heaviness of spirit—that if Barack Obama is the essay, Donald Trump is the manifesto. Trump has shown himself to be aggressive and brash, a force for polarization and an enemy of facts; his appeals are aimed not only at emotion over reason but at the very basest emotions of his cult-like base. This is the dark side of the manifesto: the side that motivates Trump's former White House Chief Strategist Steve Bannon's aggressive, nihilistic brand of disruption. To quote Margaret Atwood again—as someone who has written and signed her share of manifestos, including this one, *Am I a Bad Feminist?* (2018)—and has written about abuses of power and the threat of ideological extremism:

> In times of extremes, extremists win. Their ideology becomes a religion, anyone who doesn't puppet their views is seen as an apostate, a heretic or a traitor, and moderates in the middle are annihilated.... The aim of ideology is to eliminate ambiguity.

60. Stylistic terrorism

"To impose your ABC is a natural thing," Tzara wrote, "—therefore regrettable." Ultimately, as we are seeing, us versus them is a dangerous and destructive strategy. In one of the first scholarly treatises on the avant-garde manifesto, Lauren Shumway wrote compellingly about some of its defining features—including something she called "stylistic terrorism." (This was in 1980.) Unlike earlier manifestos, which tended to speak to the widest group possible, the avant-garde manifesto narrowed the focus considerably, isolating a small coterie, the faithful or chosen ones, from the mass of society. This select group of pledges were taught to rage against other isms and society at large, in opposition to whom they defined themselves. This played into related practices and beliefs in the modernist period, like the professionalization of the arts, the interest in the occult and hermetic knowledge, and the idea of artists as natural aristocrats (I think here of Yeats and Pound holed up in their cottage in Sussex). Shumway used the phrase "stylistic terrorism" to describe this method of marking out and solidifying a faithful group—like Pound's oft-stated desire for "a few good men" (yes, always men) to push the culture forward. In this sense Shumway's observation holds even when manifestos speak to a wider group, like Marinetti's antagonistic address to Venetians, because they still maintain a conspiratorial "we" or "us" against an undefined "you" or "them." Janet Lyon later called this tendency the "either/or configuration of the avant-garde manifesto." Unlike the essay, which in Adorno's words is "fragmentary" and "partial," the manifesto is often totalizing, and although this lends it the air of confidence and strength, it also makes it prone to hollowness, pomposity and failure. On the other hand some avant-garde manifestos—including many "anti-manifestos"—do allow elements of irony, ambiguity and ambivalence to sneak in. Dada manifestos in particular exhibit an anarchic tendency to resist or undermine aggressively doctrinaire and authoritarian behavior. Tzara writes: "I always speak of myself because I don't want to convince anyone, I don't have the right to drag others along in my current, I am not obliging anyone to follow me and everyone does his art in his own way...DADA was born of a desire for independence, of a distrust of the community." The best revolutionary and avant-garde manifestos resist replicating the traditional manifesto's bullying behavior, leading instead by example and leaving the door open to converts. This more passive and playful approach is summed up in the dazzling manifesto *Dada Excites Everything* (1921):

If you have serious ideas about life,
If you make artistic discoveries
and if all of a sudden your head begins to crackle with laughter,
if you find all your ideas useless and ridiculous, know that
IT IS DADA BEGINNING TO SPEAK TO YOU

61. Unloved and outdated

Though it was the talk of many towns a century ago, and is currently enjoying a significant renaissance among artists and activists, the manifesto has seen bad times. After the 1970s, with the shift from modernism to postmodernism, Perry Anderson argued that the manifesto had become "outdated" — "at variance with the spirit of the age." Anderson wasn't wrong: manifestos, with the exception of the most ironic self-undoing Dadaist ones, did seem out of place in an era of postmodern uncertainty. When I started reading manifestos in earnest around the turn of the millennium it was hard to think of anything less fashionable — no anthologies existed and there was next to nothing left in print. But then postmodernism itself began to fade, as all isms fade eventually, and a new spirit of "assertive purism" was born, nurtured by social media and raised on algorithmically-enhanced radicalism and a sense of endless crisis. Didn't see that coming in the tranquilized nineties, did you?

62. A pariah reborn

When I think of the manifesto's failures I think of David Gascoyne, the English Surrealist. In the 1930s, feeling simultaneously revved up by radical politics and side-lined from the excitement of the European avant-garde, as the Vorticists had been a generation before, Gascoyne wrote in his diary: "Moral bombs and dynamite are of no use whatsoever; the island's damp climate extinguishes the fuses." I also think of the poet and sometime Futurist Mina Loy, whose *Feminist Manifesto* (1914)—one of the works for which she is now most remembered—languished for decades in obscurity, unseen, until it was published posthumously in a new edition of *The Lost Lunar Baedeker* in 1982. As recently as 2008, when the Serpentine Gallery held its Manifesto Marathon, an event celebrating the centenary of the first Futurist manifesto, everyone involved seemed to be either declaring the manifesto dead or defensively acknowledging its "pariah" status (as an essay in the catalog titled "The Manifesto: What's in it for Us?" put it). A speech by the historian Eric Hobsbawm raised doubts about the continuing viability of the manifesto, seeing it as a twentieth century phenomenon, while the novelist Tom McCarthy declared it a "defunct format." (The Hate Socialist Collective began its 2009 manifesto *Leave the Manifesto Alone: A Manifesto*: "The manifesto is dead.") With friends like these, who needs enemies? Yet the organizers of the Manifesto Marathon were prescient, because immediately afterwards, owing to the confluence of a number of factors—from the financial crisis to the rise of smart phones and social media—manifestos made an unexpected and triumphant return. Just as *The Founding and Manifesto of Futurism* had graced the front page of *Le Figaro* in 1909, by the 2010s manifestos were again making headlines: from Occupy and Pussy Riot to Black Lives Matter, #MeToo and #NeverAgain. Cate Blanchett was starring in a film called *Manifesto* and Lorde was wearing one of Jenny Holzer's *Inflammatory Essays* sewn into her dress at the Grammys. The militant manifesto, once a pariah, was reborn.

63. No place

The manifesto still has its problems, of course. Anything involving a) the future, and b) utopias, for example, usually tends toward vagueness and the rehashing of old futures. The word "utopia," first used in the book by Thomas More, literally means "no place" (Greek *ou* "not" + *topos* "place"), and this no-place-ness is a weakness in many manifestos. The weakness comes in two main varieties: either the utopia described is too nice, impossibly perfect—huge societal problems are too easily and mysteriously solved—and thus it lacks both narrative stakes and relevance to our urgently troubled, nitty-gritty world; or the utopia is creepily perfect and not so nice at all: a panopticon, an eerily calm, heavily surveilled utopia, a place where nothing happens—a no chewing gum, no picnicking on the grass, no transgressions, rule-bound paradise (not unlike the biblical Eden). Georges Perec once wrote: "All utopias are depressing because they leave no room for chance, for difference, for the miscellaneous." He might have been thinking of *News From Nowhere* (1890), in which William Morris portrays an idealized retro-futuristic England, conflict-free and full of obscenely healthy, sexually liberated, rational and harmonious citizens—a sort of London as Swedish socialist summer camp. Aside from being dull, utopias of the past—especially the boom at the turn of the last century, overlapping with the rise of the avant-garde manifesto—often traded in dodgy or downright sinister ideas, including racism, eugenics, and "uses" for the poor. Manifestos from this period share the same history, and many of the same flaws.

64. Stale futures

Futures tend to go stale over time: the same old imaginaries, the same old tired dreams. This is particularly a concern in dealing with technological futures. In his book *The Shock of the Old* (2007), David Edgerton sums it up thus: "History reveals that technological futurism is largely unchanging over time. Present visions of the future display a startling, unselfconscious lack of originality." Many of the dreams of the Italian Futurists before the war—the dream of speed, the war machines—can still be seen in the dreams of techno-capitalists like Elon Musk (the Hyperloop, the flamethrower, the moon rocket). Oscar Wilde's dream of robot slaves enabling a life of leisure in *The Soul of Man Under Socialism* (1891)—"On mechanical slavery, on the slavery of the machine, the future of the world depends," he wrote—is a dream that still figures heavily in the promises of advertising, despite equally persistent evidence that leisure will always be a privilege of the rich. Then there is the problem of what Fredric Jameson called "nostalgia mode" and Franco "Bifo" Berardi termed the "slow cancellation of the future." Why do our technological dreams stagnate and repeat? Examples of recurring technological dreams are the jetpack and the flying car, or the futuristic "autonomous vehicle" that looks more or less the way cars have always looked. Faced with imminent planetary collapse, can't we do better? Manifestos, like speculative design, help us to think radically outside of incremental evolutionary models and the sort of safe predictability—the reselling of old goods—that reassures shareholders. Some manifesto dreams simply lose their luster over time, or prove difficult to realize. John Perry Barlow's dream, for example, in *A Declaration of the Independence of Cyberspace* (1996)—of an online world "where anyone, anywhere may express his or her beliefs, no matter how singular, without fear of being coerced into silence or conformity"—is not how most people would describe social media today. And Norman Bel Geddes's vision of an America connected by clean, efficient super-highways, unveiled at "Futurama," the General Motors Pavilion of the 1939 World's Fair, soon gave way to J. G. Ballard's dystopian vision of a degraded, polluting and dangerous system in *The Atrocity Exhibition* (1970) and *Crash* (1973). The flipside of Futurism is obsolescence: Marinetti recognized and embraced this built-in risk, promising that future generations would continue to overthrow the old, but obsolescence continues to haunt technological manifestos of all kinds. Perhaps this is why many manifestos choose to cast a critical eye on the past and present as much as attempting to imagine a bold new future. They emphasize the intolerable status quo, rather than bringing us a brave new world. Well, this can be a start. As James Bridle writes at the close of his recent book *New Dark Age* (2018):

> any strategy for living in the new dark age depends upon attention to the here and now, and not to the illusory promises of computational prediction, surveillance, ideology and representation. The present is always where we live and think, poised between an oppressive history and an unknowable future.

65. Whose dream, whose nightmare?

Manifestos, it should be remembered, are written from a particular point of view. Like the advertisements they often imitate, they serve a pretty strict agenda. So it is a good idea to ask: Whose future is this? Whose utopia? Whose dream, and whose nightmare? The Peter Thiel-backed techno-libertarian venture known as The Seasteading Institute, whose manifesto envisions a floating chain of "modular eco-villages" outside the jurisdiction of any nation state, is one example. The "moral imperatives" they hope to address with their utopian scheme sound noble enough: "Enrich the poor. Cure the Sick. Feed the Hungry. Clean the atmosphere. Restore the oceans. Live in balance with nature." But the darker side begins to emerge when cruise ships—cruise ships!—are cited as an inspiration. Further undermining the benevolent façade is TSI co-founder Wayne Gramlich's manifesto *Seasteading: Homesteading on the High Seas* (1998), which emphasizes "tax avoidance" as a core principle and "sea surface colonization" as the primary objective. Thiel's own manifesto, *The Education of a Libertarian* (2009), appears to blame women and the poor for the failures of democracy. He places hope for the future in "companies like Facebook" which "create the space for new modes of dissent and new ways to form communities not bounded by historical nation-states." Instead of true internationalism, Thiel seems to offer only American multinationalism and corporate colonialism. Instead of elected governments, the future will be ruled by the CEOs of private companies serving a small elite who wish to live outside the law. For the many, gated utopian visions like Seasteading promise futures as problematic and undesirable as the present we already live in. Whose future? Their future—a future for the few.

66. The beauty of failure

"It does not matter if it is a failure," Derek Jarman wrote in a manifesto from his student days in the early 1960s. "Failures are to be desired as long as they are complete, stretched to their limits." Near the end of his life, in *Modern Nature*, his diary of 1989-90 when he was already living with HIV/AIDS, Jarman revisits the theme of failure as seen in a positive light. He writes about tending his garden on the barren shores of Dungeness, on the south coast of England, in a way that resonates with the hope and hopelessness of writing manifestos, whose utopian ideas and initiatives are almost always doomed to failure: "I water the roses and wonder whether I will see them bloom. I plant my herbal garden as a panacea...and know they are not going to help...Yet there is a thrill in watching the plants spring up that gives me hope." Despite Tom McCarthy's criticism of the manifesto as "a defunct format" in 2008, the novelist admitted being attracted to its anachronistic style, its "bombast and aggression." "Things that don't work have great potential," he wrote, comparing the manifesto to Duchamp's "broken bicycle wheel." If you agree with McCarthy—and it's hard not to see the retro charm of the avant-garde—that is another way to find the manifesto useful even in its failure. (Bruce Sterling's *Dead Media Manifesto* from the mid-1990s, which called for a "media book of the dead," used the "defunct format" to champion other victims of obsolescence.) Aside from that, there is always the chance your manifesto might *not* fail. Beyond the mountains of wreckage, the broken promises and faded dreams, there are successes too. These include everything from Imagist poems and Futurist paintings to women's suffrage, workers' rights, LGBTQ rights, the rights of visible minorities, and whole nations freed from the political and cultural shackles of their colonizers. When they succeed, manifestos make powerful examples of putting ideas into action. Even when they fail, the radical visions they present can be a source of inspiration for the future.

67. Weakness is strength

Sometimes, as in the case of Valerie Solanas, the charm or magic of a manifesto is in its potent mix of strength and vulnerability — the sense of being marginalized by society, but wearing the mask of strength and performing power. In this sense, failure is not a negative attribute. Without the underlying weakness, the show of strength would lose its poignancy and potency, becoming meaningless. In fact this type of failure is present in many of the most compelling manifestos. The failure is to show no weakness, no humanity or humility or empathy. Some manifestos show failings or blind spots, a surfeit of negative emotions like anger or violence, but if they show redeeming qualities like humor and self-awareness there is hope. Fragility and ephemerality do not in themselves constitute failure. But they are close enough to the risk of failure to lend manifestos a sense of drama, and to make any modest success in achieving their far-fetched dreams seem extraordinary. Handling manifestos in the archive, feeling the delicate flaky yellow paper of their crumbling edges, you get the feeling that they have survived almost by accident, or at least against great odds. Some manifestos, it is true, are written with a larger sense of history in mind, and with the wish to make a permanent mark. Most, however, think only of making changes in the present. In that circumscribed but noble wish (depending on the ends they hope to achieve) lies a great deal of their power and beauty.

Futures

68. Here comes the future

The first "manifesto moment," according to the scholar and translator Mary Ann Caws, happened in the 1910s. The second moment occurred half a century later, in the 1960s, fostered by the neo-avant-garde and widespread social upheaval. The third—digital—manifesto moment has been gathering momentum, right on schedule, throughout the 2010s. The start of the latest wave of manifesto writing could be set, somewhat arbitrarily but not without reason, at 2008: a year that, like Woolf's birth of modernism "on or about December 1910," saw the real arrival of the digital age with the rise of the iPhone and social media, new networks and new habits of reading, making and sharing, not to mention—as the economic crisis hit, and its effects began to reverberate across the globe—the pervasive, media-fed atmosphere of mass confusion and unrelenting crisis that we still live in today. According to Nicholas Mirzoeff, who writes eloquently about such big picture concerns, 2008 was also the first time in history that more people lived in cities than in the countryside, which may be relevant to the manifesto's significant urban bias. Barack Obama was elected in 2008, partly with the help of Shepard Fairey's iconic *Hope* poster. If more weight is needed to make 2008 the tipping point for the rebirth of the manifesto, October of that year also saw the Manifesto Marathon hosted at the Serpentine Gallery in London, curated by Hans Ulrich Obrist and others, in the temporary Pavilion designed by Frank Gehry. Manifesto performers included Marina Abramović, Yoko Ono, Ai Weiwei, Vivienne Westwood, Agnès Varda, Jonas Mekas, Eric Hobsbawm, Rem Koolhaas, Stewart Home, Gilbert and George, Brian Eno and many others. The Marathon's own manifesto declared, in a typical speech act (make it so!): "At this moment, there is a reconnection to the manifesto as a document of poetic and political intent." The Marathon also marked the centenary of *The Founding and Manifesto of Futurism*, written in the autumn of 1908 and published in *Le Figaro* on February 20, 1909—followed soon afterwards by numerous other commemorations in academic and artistic circles. Manifestos and emerging technologies have always gone hand in hand: for Futurism this meant everything from new media (radio, cinema, press) to transportation (the celebrated automobile, airplanes).

69. Futures thinking

Thinking about and shaping (manifesting) the future are two of the manifesto's principal tasks. In the best cases the two things go together:

future vision + practical social/artistic application = manifesto

If you want a glimpse of future visions over the past two hundred years or so, manifestos, like science fiction, are a good place to look. Admittedly they tend actually to be as much or more about the present than the future (also like sci-fi), but they are still a better place than most to find out what original thinkers—artists, architects, designers or activists—wanted from the future, and how they thought they might get it. It may seem an obvious point, but other animals don't write manifestos. Humans create all sorts of extraordinary tools to change their environment. One thing humans are not so good at, however, is long-term thinking. It's worth recognizing how rare it actually is to think actively and creatively about the future. Where I live, in Portugal, public employees' pay is divided into 14 instead of 12 months, with double paychecks coming in June (for summer holidays) and December (for Christmas, presumably). When I moved here I found this system patronizing—I didn't need the government telling me how to spend my money! But I soon realized that I was having trouble saving anything beyond the last day of each month. When the "extra" paycheck arrived twice a year, I needed it. And when the government took the thirteenth and fourteenth paychecks away during the financial crisis, I protested with my fellow public sector workers—a good example, as I see it, of how we tend to think reactively rather than proactively.

70. Build the future you want

In his bright little book *The Future*, Nick Montfort talks about active "future-making" — that, "The future is not something to be predicted, but to be made." One of his examples is the manifesto, which raises active future-making over passive future viewing or receiving. The futures conceived in manifestos like those of Italian Futurism — however far out — help us to think actively and critically, hopefully avoiding disappointing futures, stale imaginaries and what twenty-first century futurist Scott Smith calls "flat-pack futures": those prefabricated, mundane, repetitive, even sinister futures that are wholly inadequate to the political, environmental, artistic and existential challenges we face. Like speculative design, manifestos help us to think outside of narrow futures. They help us to imagine radically and not just incrementally different futures. Manifesto thinking is the Futurists' complete overhaul of Italian cuisine, or the opening up of language to create "words in freedom."

71. Resist dominant futures

Manifestos are important because they show concern for the future. As I mentioned above, humans have always been poor at futures thinking—but manifestos are an exception. They help us build alternatives, or simply resist dominant futures. They help us to think outside of neoliberalism, for example, which is something a lot of people increasingly want—and something that is urgently needed from an ecological standpoint. In *Against Amazon: Seven Arguments, One Manifesto* (2017), the Spanish writer Jorge Carrión argues that we must resist the future Amazon represents—in terms of literary culture, consumption and working conditions—even if we inevitably give in at times, and even if resistance seems futile because "theirs is the music of the world." "We are all cyborgs," he writes, "But we don't want to be robots." He argues that we can use the logic and innovations of platform capitalism against itself, mixing up categories and blurring lines: "Let there be bottles of Argentinian wine next to the complete works of Borges." Resistance, even if it is small in scale, is not futile. *The Maker's Bill of Rights*, first published in 2005 and updated by Garnet Hertz in 2018, takes the form of a list of vows intended to shape the future of the Maker Movement by correcting its present trajectory and obvious weaknesses. The new edition includes examples like: "If women don't have a pivotal voice at an event, panel or exhibition, I'm not participating. I will not participate in hackathons that exploit talent for free ideas. I have a right to be paid for my creative and technical work." Such vows represent active steps that, if taken, *will* change the future.

72. Speculative propositions

At the same time, a key aspect of manifesto writing is walking the line between fiction and reality, provocation and practical change. Central to the platform of the Laboria Cuboniks collective's striking manifesto *Xenofeminism: A Politics for Alienation* (2015) is a call for gender abolitionism—a radical proposal on the face of it, although it is carefully unpacked in the manifesto itself: "'Gender abolitionism' is shorthand for the ambition to construct a society where traits currently assembled under the rubric of gender, no longer furnish a grid for the asymmetric operation of power." As one member of the collective later admitted, the abolition of gender was "a speculative proposition"—easier to proclaim wearing the manifesto's mask, perhaps, than to explain in the context of a podcast interview wearing the hat of an academic. But radical speculation and attention-grabbing ideas have an important role to play. Just as exploring the possible futures of DIY surgery through speculative design (as Frank Kolkman did in his OpenSurgery project) is a worthwhile venture for the questions it raises—while not necessarily being a "how to" guide—so you don't have to literally abolish gender to make a point about gender inequality, or destroy museums and libraries to acknowledge the point of the first Futurist manifesto: that centuries of history and culture weigh too heavily on young artists, and that art has to be recognized as a living entity as well as a form of heritage or patrimony. Manifestos are testing grounds for radical new ideas.

73. Problematic futures

Like the angel in Walter Benjamin's *Theses on the Philosophy of History* (1940), hurtling backward into the future as he watches the storm of progress "piling wreckage upon wreckage" at his feet, when we look at the manifesto's past futures it is possible to see only failures. So many problematic futures—racist, misogynistic, technophilic, warmongering—so little self-awareness. Sensitivity has never been the manifesto's strong suit: it is often used as a blunt instrument, a hammer to deliver the message. Even where we least expect it—for example in Mina Loy's *Feminist Manifesto*, which offers so much to celebrate—there are lines that should make us recoil, such as: "Every woman of superior intelligence should realize her race-responsibility, in producing children in adequate proportion to the unfit or degenerate members of her sex." I still love Loy's manifesto, or find *much to love in it*—as I do Valentine de Saint-Point's *Futurist Manifesto of Lust* (1913), which seems (if taken literally) to endorse rape by soldiers in battle. Or Marinetti's manifestos, despite their calls to invade Abyssinia, set fire to libraries and heap scorn on women. Or the Vorticist magazine *BLAST*, despite its homophobic jokes, its hate-filled poems by Pound and its patronizing plea to Suffragettes to "leave works of art alone." (Most manifestos written before 1970 display at the very least a casual sexism, leaving half the population out of their future plans.) It's not always easy to love manifestos. It requires a compartmentalization of mind that is difficult to manage and even more difficult, at times impossible, to defend. That the same could be said for other genres, where the evidence might be less obviously on display, doesn't change the fact: manifestos are problematic.

74. Faring better

Some past futures inevitably hold up better than others. The worst you can say about *transition* magazine's *The Revolution of the Word*, for example, is that it smacks of elitism ("The plain reader be damned")—a charge that could be leveled at most modernist manifestos. As in the Futurist manifestos, *transition* calls for a future in which time is somehow abolished, and language is set free. There are numerous postcolonial manifestos that inspire with their vision of a culturally and politically independent future, such as the Brazilian poet Oswald de Andrade's *Cannibalist Manifesto* (1928) or the Nigerian artist Uche Okeke's *Natural Synthesis* manifesto (1960), which begins: "Young artists in a new nation, that is what we are!" Lucio Fontana's *White Manifesto* (1946) is interesting as an early attempt to unite art and science, calling on research scientists to help artists develop a truly modern art form. Also faring well over time are the technical manifestos, which stick to lecturing on craft elements in specific disciplines such as painting, poetry, music, architecture, film or design, and thus avoid getting embroiled in (and dated by) wider political debates.

75. No more ambiguity

Manifestos that have had a lasting impact on their field through their future visions are too numerous to mention—that is the nature and *raison d'être* of most manifestos. But it is worth noting and rather curious that two manifestos, far above any others, still serve as the principal templates for manifesto writing in the twenty-first century: *The Communist Manifesto* and *The Founding and Manifesto of Futurism*. An entire study has been written on the influence of the former; the influence of the latter is still evident in the structure and tone of almost every avant-garde manifesto written today. The Freee Art Collective launched a *New Futurist Manifesto* on the centenary in 2009 at the Institute of Contemporary Arts in London. Written over the top of and thus in direct dialog with the original, it is both an updated version and a reflection on manifesto style, how and why manifestos are written, and the function of polemical writing generally. One of the tenets of this manifesto states, echoing the Futurists but responding to the twenty-first century London art scene: "No more ambiguity! No more irony! No more pussy-footing-around! Artists, it is time to say something and stand by what you say!"

76. Space for desire

The centenary exhibition of Futurism at the Museum of Modern Art in New York perfectly described the manifesto as an "entrepreneurial method of mass promotion." With this medium, in concert with their experiments across various disciplines, "the Futurists freed expression from the bounds of tradition and propriety." The rest is history. The Futurist visions of Italy—visions in which the canals of Venice would be filled in with the rubble of its buildings, everything razed flat and rebuilt from the ground up—were reflected in the Fascist architecture of the interwar period, especially in colonial outposts such as Asmara in Eritrea, as well as in postwar poetry experiments and other artistic innovations. But the legacy of Futurism is seen above all in the avant-garde manifesto and the militant art movement. There is a basic contradiction in many manifestos in the sense that they are nostalgic, even reactionary in their visions of the future. Like utopian narratives generally, they often look backward in order to look ahead. But sometimes their backward-looking seems valid, even particularly modern or relevant, as in these lines from a poetic manifesto by the filmmaker Agnès Varda in 2008:

Is it sometimes progress to go backwards?
Back to the basic needs,
Plus space for desire

We can always learn from the past, while at the same time resisting the seduction of empty promises and shiny plastic futures—but we must also avoid the pitfalls of nostalgia and the eternal return, the faded dreams of past futures.

77. New networks of distribution

In the old days manifesto distribution meant posters, pamphlets and cabaret performances. As usual, Marinetti's Futurists went to the greatest extremes—perhaps the best example being the publication of *Against Traditionalist Venice*. As Marinetti himself describes it (possibly with a hint of numerical inflation): "On July 8, 1910, 800,000 leaflets containing this manifesto were hurled by the Futurist poets and painters from the top of the Clock Tower onto the crowds returning from the Lido. Thus began the campaign." Marinetti's tactic was imitated by Lars von Trier in 1995, when after reading out the Dogme manifesto on stage at a film symposium he threw handfuls of red leaflets into the audience. In other cases the Futurists threw manifestos from speeding cars or shouted them from the stage at Futurist "evenings," where they encouraged the audience to hurl abuse and rotten vegetables. Manifesto poster art reached its apogee in the counterculture and second-wave avant-garde of the 1960s: seen for example in the slogan-based posters printed by the *Atelier Populaire* during the events of May 1968, or the Black Panthers' image of Bobby Seale in the electric chair. Although in our century print media, street art and physical protests continue to hold power, a new world of digital networks and dissemination has also opened up. I've discovered this while writing various born-digital manifestos with people all over the world. Two manifestos I wrote for an online literary journal— one about writing, which appears in a slightly different form at the beginning of this book, and another against Fascism, which was made to be printed out and pasted up in physical locations—were collaborations between an Argentina-born graphic designer in Los Angeles, an American editor living in London, and myself, an Irish-Canadian living in Portugal. Who was their readership? Hardly anyone! It was a little magazine.

Yet the readership was also anyone and everyone, since unlike the avant-garde print magazines of a century ago, which cost money and were only sold in specialty shops in big cities, it was free and online, and could pop up in anyone's feed.

78. Children living at the end of the world

In 2017 the Canadian artist Grimes used Instagram and Tumblr to launch a new music genre. The posts had an audience of more than a million followers, and the Tumblr post included what she called "the first paragraph of my manifesto." It began: "The fae are the children living at the end of the world, who make art that reflects what its [sic] like to live knowing the earth may not sustain humanity much longer." It's a decent start to a manifesto, self-defining and suitably apocalyptic. The manifesto was accompanied by a playlist and an image drawn by Grimes in her usual faerie-anime-graffiti style. (The official Instagram account for Grimes's visual art uses Marx as the avatar.) Comments, hundreds of them, appeared below the posts. The manifesto reached a lot of people. Inevitably one day social media will die or be superseded beyond recognition, as will mobile phones. ("We want it to happen!" as the Futurists would say.) The manifesto, if the last 2 centuries are anything to go by, will continue to adapt and thrive, always using the latest technology to channel its future-oriented demands, illustrating William Gibson's idea that "the street finds its own uses for things."

79. Context collapse

Have the new modes of dissemination and expression changed the manifesto itself? Yes, although exactly how is a complex question. One major shift is what has been called "context collapse." When isms went to war a century ago, they were fighting on solid ground. They shared the same vocabulary and similar points of reference. The dissolution of this context means you now need to shout even louder to be heard. It also means that you are less sure of who you are shouting at, and you're more likely to be misunderstood. The journalist Quinn Norton used context collapse as her defense in an essay-manifesto published in *The Atlantic* in February 2018, titled *"The New York Times* Fired My Doppelgänger." The essay was a response to being unceremoniously fired over controversial opinions revealed in past tweets. Norton states: "I was accused of homophobia because of the in-group language I used with anons when I worked with them. ('Anons' refers to people who identify as part of the activist collective Anonymous.)" The end of Norton's essay gestures strongly toward manifesto style in its sweeping vision of the present and our navigation of possible futures: "No one prepared us for this, no one trained us, no one came before us with an understanding of our world. ...We have to build our own philosophies and imagine great futures for our world in order to have any futures at all." When she was fired some people sympathized with her, while many others did not. The same thing almost happened again at *The Times* a few months later with the hiring of Sarah Jeong. In this case the allegations, based on old tweets dug up by far-right trolls, failed to stick.

80. Pressure by design

The Silicon Valley sage-cum-critic Jaron Lanier has written several manifestos about our relationship with technology, including *One-Half of a Manifesto* (2000), *You Are Not a Gadget: A Manifesto* (2010) and *Ten Arguments for Deleting Your Social Media Accounts Right Now* (2018). In his latest book Lanier discusses not only the perils of context collapse but also the way in which algorithms encourage us to stick to a limited number of groups and issues, reinforcing our sense of identity every time we go online. This is good for the manifesto, in a sense, but it is bad for individual and critical thought. On the positive side, as Lanier points out, algorithms can help build support. Movements like the Arab Spring or Black Lives Matter or #MeToo might not have happened without the visibility and sheer force of numbers afforded by social media acceleration. The same could be true, however, for the rise of so-called white nationalism or Islamic State. Also with social media comes the constant push—pressure by design—to form and declare strong opinions, to argue with opponents, to give voice to negative feelings and outrage—all as a means of soliciting and securing content and engagement for the platform itself.

81. Acceleration and reaction

Understandably, there has been a backlash against the pace of technological innovation and the lack of control we often feel as a result. A century ago the Vorticists scoffed at Futurism's enthusiasm for the latest technologies. In the opening manifesto of *BLAST* they affected a seen-it-all-before world weariness: "AUTOMOBILISM (Marinetteism) bores us...Wilde gushed twenty years ago about the beauty of machinery." Since the 1990s one reaction has been Accelerationism, which basically calls for the acceleration of capitalism's already breakneck tempo, either to revel in it (on the Right) or to bring about its early demise (on the Left). There are various kinds of neo-Luddite responses too, such as the 2017 arson of the Casemate fablab in Grenoble, France. In their manifesto issued after the attack, the self-described anarchists declared: "our communiqué [is] an inseparable echo of our incendiary act against this institution which is notoriously harmful for its diffusion of digital culture." The "slow" movement is another reaction. Following the *Slow Food Manifesto* (1989) and the *Slow Media Manifesto* (2010), Vincenzo Di Nicola's *Slow Thought: A Manifesto* (2018) elucidates seven principles, including the practice of being "asynchronic" or resisting the speed of modern times in favor of "the slow logic of thought" and working toward greater focus.

82. Open and free

One thing I've noticed reading a lot of manifestos from the past 2 decades is that the majority seem to be concerned with openness, whether it is making information free or exposing injustices by bringing them to light. In *A Hacker Manifesto* (2004), McKenzie Wark reframes as his epigraph Microsoft CEO Steve Ballmer's description of the appeal of the internet: "it sort of springs organically from the earth. And it has the characteristics of communism, that people love so very much about it. That is, it's free." Wark argues that, "Hackers create the possibility of new things entering the world. Not always great things, or even good things, but new things." The people who write manifestos on behalf of a free and open internet are passionate about wanting to keep it that way, from Barlow's *A Declaration of the Independence of Cyberspace* in the 1990s to the *European Pirate Party Manifesto* in the 2010s, which aims to defend the internet "as a common good and a public utility": neutral, open access and copyright free for non-commercial use. Some of these texts are included in an anthology called *Manifestos for the Internet Age*, which first appeared in 2015. The book's production values reflect the broader culture it represents. Published by Greyscale Press, it was "generated" by an anonymous collective over a single weekend. It is still a work in progress—my paper copy is beta version 0.7. Participation in future iterations is encouraged, which means that infinite changes and additions are possible. In this sense it realizes the old modernist dream, expressed in the circular form of James Joyce's *Finnegans Wake* (aka "Work in Progress"). The end circles back to the beginning—"a way a lone a last a loved a long the / riverrun, past Eve and Adam's, from swerve of shore to bend of bay"—and Finnegan begins again, like the potentially endless emendations and extensions written into galley proofs of Joyce's previous book, *Ulysses*, which really only stopped because of Joyce's love for numerology and his wish to have a copy printed in time for his fortieth birthday. So everything is a work in progress, an endless draft. In so many ways we are only just now catching up to Joyce, which would have surprised no one less than the author himself. "Laugh at perfection," as the eighth tenet of *The Cult of Done Manifesto* (2009) commands us. I have taken this advice to heart in composing the book you are reading now. But is this approach really wise? If everything now exists forever, should we not work for a greater rather than a lesser degree of finish? How much more half-baked content does the world need? On the other hand, instability and iteration are as much a part of internet culture as openness—as V2_'s *Manifesto for the Unstable Media* (1987) makes clear. "Though an historical document," the manifesto nevertheless will need "continuous updating, being, as it should be, unstable." Quite so!

83. Making manifest vs. keeping crypto

Something notable about digital manifestos is the frequent blurring and overlap between theory and action, the virtual and the real. This has long been the case with manifestos, of course: Futurism and other movements frequently sought to cross the line into real life. Since the 1960s examples of violent action supported by violent rhetoric have become almost common, from Valerie Solanas and Ted Kaczynski to Anders Breivik and Dylann Roof. Thankfully most digital manifestos are utopian in spirit and at least ostensibly intended to serve the greater good. Edward Snowden's *A Manifesto for the Truth*, for example, originally published in German in *Der Spiegel*, lays out the principles behind his decision to leak classified information on surveillance activities by the National Security Agency in 2013. Aaron Swartz, who committed suicide that same year, aged 26, while facing a US federal indictment for data theft, left a record of his idealistic views in the *Guerilla Open Access Manifesto* (2008). There has always been another central paradox too: between bringing to light, or making manifest, and keeping hidden, or "crypto." The early avant-gardes were as drawn to occult practices and secret societies as they were to publishing their aims before the world. Self-proclaimed "crypto-anarchists" like Defense Distributed founder Cody Wilson are a recent variation on this tendency. For years Wilson has used manifestos and manifesto-like statements as part of his public relations campaign to spread the availability of digital plans for private gun manufacture. (His first video manifesto was released in March 2013.) Wilson's project is also relevant to the manifesto because it is primarily intended as a provocation—probing a possible future—as he stated in a debate at the "Design and Violence" exhibition at MoMA in 2014. "I'm trying to controversialize it," Wilson said. "My project works because it's uncompromising, it's abrasive...I'm not trying to sell you something." While that last part may not be true, Wilson is successful in manifesto terms because he paints a complex vision of the future, beyond practical capabilities (but as if the dream was completely within reach), and encapsulates a whole future in a brief text and image. For years his PR has been better than his legal progress, but in June 2018 the US State Department decided in Wilson's favor, accepting his argument that code was a form of speech (and therefore covered under the First Amendment) and allowing him to publish weapons data on the internet. This decision was temporarily blocked after a public outcry about so-called "ghost guns"—and Wilson has run into other legal problems since—but the broader issue is far from resolved.

84. New language

What do manifestos sound like in the twenty-first century? Many sound more or less the same, since they use the same templates (Moses, Marx and Marinetti). But the shifts happening to language on the internet more broadly also impact manifesto writing, possibly to a disproportionate degree given the natural affinities between manifestos and social media. Twitter is an obvious example: if you use the platform regularly, as a lot of writers do, in effect you're already fluent in *manifesto-ese*. You are conditioned to make your point as clearly and directly as possible, to find and push forward a strong "take" on any issue, and to win converts with emotional, gut-level appeals. We are more competitive than ever, projecting arrogance as we shout to be heard in the crowded marketplace of ideas. In the process we expand the Overton window, the sense of what is acceptable in polite discourse. It might be wise to ask: is this desirable? The aphoristic, elliptical language once used in poetry and manifestos has become our everyday language online—and vice-versa, since this online language mutates and feeds back into art. Joyce and Stein took us halfway there, but the other half has been the influence of the digital age. Toby Litt uses the phrase "sentence confetti" ("single sentences, isolated by meaningful space") to describe "the default form of contemporary, post-internet writing." Fragmentary style can be seen in countless recent examples such as Maggie Nelson's *Bluets* (2009), Lucy Corin's *One Hundred Apocalypses and Other Apocalypses* (2016), Sarah Manguso's *300 Arguments* (2017) and Joanna Walsh's *Break.up* (2018). The American poet and provocateur Kenneth Goldsmith has argued for years that social media and messaging is not killing language but making it better and more poetic—and making us better, more avid and more critical in our reading. We invent and reinvent ourselves constantly, declaring and defending our principles in public with every tweet and disappearing message—as fleeting as the Futurists predicted, as epigrammatic and enigmatic as Wilde could have hoped.

85. Everything is a manifesto

In what could be either a throwaway provocation or a sign that we've reached peak manifesto, an Egyptian artist known as Ganzeer recently declared: "It's time everything was a manifesto." Ganzeer came to prominence as a young street artist during the 2011 Egyptian Revolution. The line comes from *Manifesto Everything* (2018), and in fact it raises an interesting point: that everything should be made or done with purpose and intention in our increasingly wasteful and oversaturated age. He asks: "What if every single human act was backed by a manifesto...would we still be making shit?" Ironically it is capitalism that has promoted the idea in recent years that everything needs a manifesto — "manifesto" in this sense being an edgier name for "business plan" or "mission statement." "Why You Should Write a Manifesto For Everything You Do" is the typical sort of business-related article you find in a Google search for manifestos nowadays. Unintentionally (or not?) echoing the first Futurist manifesto, the article begins: "We all dream of our manifesto moment, when we write all night..." ("We stayed up all night, my friends and I...").

86. What's Goop?

Manifestos for business might be inspiring, visionary, even in some sense provocative, but they can never be anything less than positive—the manifesto as boosterism, techno-capitalist utopianism. Which brings us to Goop. The mission statement of Gwyneth Paltrow's aspirational lifestyle company is, like most corporate statements for new media companies, a kind of manifesto. "What's Goop?" begins every point in its platform with "We"; it uses familiar manifesto phrases such as, "We believe" and "We know who we are; our words and actions are aligned." It also provides the kind of origin narrative often found in a manifesto's preamble: "Launched in the fall of 2008 out of Gwyneth Paltrow's kitchen as a homespun weekly newsletter..." The timing is worth noting, since it was at that exact moment that the global economic crisis hit. I remember it vividly because it was the month I moved from Canada to Portugal, and every year I spent in Lisbon for the next five was worse than the one before, as austerity bit deeper and protests by students and pensioners and public sector workers grew larger and more desperate, even violent. Cobblestones were thrown and flaming barricades were built in the streets around the parliament. Occupy Wall Street was happening. Students were rioting in London. Greece burned. Goop thrived. Suddenly everything truly was a manifesto.

87. Renewal! Renewal!

The spirit of revolution, rebirth, renewal, change; the leading edge, hope of tomorrow, the avant-garde, the advent of the new world out of the destruction of the old. As Blaise Cendrars wrote in *The ABCs of Cinema* (1917-21), a giddy manifesto inspired by the possibilities of the new form: "Watch the new generations growing up suddenly like flowers. Revolution. Youth of the world. Today." The manifesto is above all a youthful genre—no other comes close in this regard. It is full of confidence, curiosity, energy, idealism, foolishness, flamboyance and fundamentalism. It is impatient for action and change. The *SCUM Manifesto* (1967) declares: "SCUM is impatient." *The Mundane Afrofuturist Manifesto* (2013) ends with a vow: "To burn this manifesto as soon as it gets boring." Manifestos are mostly written by the young, like the editorial staff of *The Eagle Eye*, the student newspaper of Marjorie Stoneman Douglas High School, who published *Our Manifesto to Fix America's Gun Laws* in *The Guardian* in 2018. Or the Italian Futurists, who boasted in their first manifesto: "The oldest of us is thirty." (Marinetti was actually 31.) Tristan Tzara was only 21 when he wrote the *Dada Manifesto* of 1918. So was Mayakovsky when he wrote the Russian Futurist manifesto *We, Too, Want Meat!* in 1914, with its opening provocation: "Soldiers! I envy you! You have it good!" Not to be ageist: manifestos can be written by anyone for any reason, and many are written by artists or activists in their thirties, forties, fifties and beyond. Sometimes you need the experience or the broader perspective that comes with age. Sometimes it takes until your thirties to be sufficiently fed up with the status quo. But when you write a manifesto—I say this from personal experience—it helps to put on the unlined mask of youth when you speak, channeling all the exuberance and egotism and reckless vitality of that age.

88. Manifestos in an age of post-truth

The Parkland students' manifesto is a good example of activism and manifesto writing in the US since 2016 for several reasons: the combination of online and real-world action, the manifesto's return to prominence and relevance, the new militancy of youth movements, and the questioning of what can and can't be challenged in public. In the digital context, manifestos provide both a model and a warning: on one hand, they show us how to inhabit a direct, critical, public voice; on the other, they are prone to all the familiar online traps of propaganda, dumbing down, "fake news" and aggressive behavior. The Parkland manifesto pushes back against the nihilistic, hollow-eyed rhetoric of manifestos by young mass shooters like Dylann Roof and Elliot Rodger, replacing it with utopian ideals and proposals for democratic change. At the same time, there is a danger in reusing old resistance tropes in uncritical ways. In her own manifesto of sorts, *Art Won't Save Us* (2018), the New York-based cultural critic and self-proclaimed "shitposter" Anna Khachiyan highlights—and in a sense also signifies—the need for caution and criticality. She is wary of the "corny wordplay and vapid sloganeering" that marked the initial response to the Trump presidency (e.g. Marilyn Minter's "PUSSY GRABS BACK" and Barbara Kruger's "PRUMP/TUTIN"), and she cites Angela Nagle's argument in *Kill All Normies* (2017) that as the alt-right borrows strategies from the New Left and politics moves beyond clear binaries, things generally are becoming a lot more complicated. Khachiyan's last point is especially important to keep in mind regarding manifestos—that while Trump makes a satisfying enemy, "Any truly serious political project to emerge from the art world" should take "a long, hard look at its own participation in platform capitalism instead of seeking solace in rehashing the battles of the past."

89. Still not surprised

If you happened to watch the Grammy Awards in 2018 or you followed the aftermath on social media, you might have noticed an unlikely intrusion by the manifesto. I live in Europe, so it was broadcast at 4am and the commentary was in Portuguese. But the next day I saw that the singer Lorde had made a statement by wearing one of Jenny Holzer's *Inflammatory Essays* — the one that begins, "Rejoice! Our times are intolerable" — stitched into her blood red dress. It struck me as a nice act of provocation. I never tire of seeing all the Holzer manifestos and slogans (from *Truisms*) on t-shirts and posters and memes nowadays, because they all seem fresh and fitting, right at home in our angry, media saturated, post-truth times. One of the most commonly reproduced slogans is "Abuse of power comes as no surprise" — which inspired its own "Not Surprised" movement and manifesto, a #MeToo-offshoot in the art world, described by its authors as "a rallying cry: a moment to come together and to speak out, loudly and in public." I have noticed, however, that some of the more unsettling texts by Holzer are reproduced and retweeted a lot less often than others. The one that starts "Don't talk down to me" has passed into the mainstream despite its shocking violence, because of its seemingly straightforward message about the oppressed fighting back against the oppressor. But others you don't see nearly as much, like the one that begins: "You get amazing sensations from guns. You get results from guns. Man is an aggressive animal..." Or another that begins "Repressing sex urges is so bad...," which seems to predict the "incel" movement and its manifestos in the toxic blend of misogynistic violence and self-pity. Holzer's text closes with the chilling line: "It's better to volunteer than to get forced." Holzer was, of course, making art *from* manifestos — yet her statements are so powerful that some of the pieces are repurposed as actual manifestos. But the inherent and intentional ambiguity of Holzer's texts makes this conversion a dangerous business, and opens the user to one of the most seductive aspects of manifestos and slogans: the temptation to fling out powerful words that have no precise meaning, or whose meaning shifts dramatically according to context, but which nevertheless impress or hurt or satisfy in the short term — with the danger of adding more blunt and divisive rhetoric to the decontextualized soup of online discourse. It is worth noting that since 2016 Holzer has adopted a more unambiguous and straightforward approach to art and activism, seen for example in her installation *Anti-Gun Truck* (2018).

90. Rules of engagement

Was there a manifesto for #MeToo? While there are numerous texts (legal, journalistic, social media) related to the movement against sexual harassment and assault that went viral in 2017, no single statement can claim to speak for the movement as a whole. The art world offshoot, We Are Not Surprised, perhaps being more familiar with the history of issuing manifesto-like statements, did release two statements in late 2017 and early 2018. (The second manifesto begins: "Three months later, WANS is still NOT SURPRISED.") In the slow build up that preceded the flood of allegations against Harvey Weinstein, New York University art student Emma Sulkowicz's protest and senior thesis project *Mattress Performance (Carry That Weight)* (2014-15) now looks like an important milestone. The durational performance piece included a manifesto of sorts: the "Rules of Engagement" that were painted on the walls of her university studio. The rules—similar to manifestos comprised of vows or constraints—take the form of a numbered list specifying materials and conduct, such as: "I may not seek help carrying the mattress." When #MeToo went viral in 2017, that momentum encouraged its spread to other areas of society and to other countries. In France the local movement ("#Balancetonporc") was met with a high profile "anti-manifesto"—a letter in *Le Monde* on January 9, 2018. The letter was co-authored by five women (Sarah Chiche, Catherine Millet, Catherine Robbe-Grillet, Peggy Sastre and Abnousse Shalmani) and signed by a "collective" of a hundred other prominent French women including Catherine Deneuve—mostly older women, as many younger feminists were quick to point out, calling attention to a generational divide. The manifesto seems to encourage this sense of a divide, in fact, as it states: "we don't recognize ourselves in this feminism that, beyond the denunciation of abuses of power, takes the face of a hatred of men and sexuality," and it endorses heteronormative male behavior at the start by using terms like "gallantry." One interesting thing to note about this manifestation and reaction, aside from the high profile return of polemical warfare, is the structure itself: the inflammatory language ("witch hunts"), the call and response, attack and counter-attack—which may in some cases be productive in moving an issue forward as well as feeding broader debates around (in this case) sex and gender, boundary lines, institutional power, free speech and so on. Or it may simply further divide society along simplistic us/them lines.

91. A potted history

The feminist manifesto has a history as long as the revolutionary manifesto itself. Olympe de Gouges's *Declaration of the Rights of Woman and of the Female Citizen*, for example, was published in 1791 with the aim of bringing to light the failures of the French Revolution in the area of women's rights. The following year Mary Wollenstonecraft (mother of Mary Shelley) published *A Vindication of the Rights of Woman* (1792), which would later be a primary influence on the Suffragette movement in Britain and North America. All this was against the backdrop of the pamphlet wars raging in those countries during the revolutionary period. First-wave feminism at the start of the twentieth century coincided with the first-wave avant-garde, and there are interesting crossovers and similarities to be found between them, including examples such as Valentine de Saint-Point's *Manifesto of Futurist Woman* (1912) and Mina Loy's *Feminist Manifesto* (1914), both written under the dual (and somewhat paradoxical) influences of feminism and Futurism. Modernist authors like Virginia Woolf and Gertrude Stein also played an important role from this period through the 1930s. Second-wave feminism brought many more examples, of course, from Valerie Solanas's *SCUM Manifesto* (1967) to the *Redstockings Manifesto* (1969) to Monique Wittig's *Combat for the Liberation of Woman* and the Third World Women's Alliance *Black Women's Manifesto* (1970). (Janet Lyon dives into this material in far greater detail than I can here in her chapter "A Second-Wave Problematic: How to Be a Radical" in *Manifestoes: Provocations of the Modern*). Third-wave feminism began in the early 1990s with manifestos such as Kathleen Hanna's *Riot Grrrl Manifesto* (1991) and Zoe Leonard's 1992 poem-manifesto *I want a president* (inspired by Eileen Myles' run for president that year as an "openly female" candidate). The fourth-wave, which began in the early 2010s with the rise of social media, and for which the manifesto has continued to play a key part, is still very much unfolding as I write.

.

92. Feminist futures

The manifesto generally had something of a wilderness phase or a lost generation between the social and artistic upheavals of the 1960s and the new energy of the internet in the mid-1990s. One example is Neoism: the *Neoist Manifesto* of 1979, which is just a defaced, unreadable text (the only legible words are "Neoism has no manifesto"), suggests that things had already more or less run their course by the late 1970s. Almost 2 decades later, when Lars von Trier launched the *Dogme 95 Manifesto* and *Vow of Chastity* on red leaflets, the genre was clearly growing tired, relying on the ironic reiteration of already ironic first- and second-wave avant-garde tropes. There were exceptions, however—the most striking of which came from the broadly feminist perspective. Responding, as women have done since Valentine de Saint-Point and Mina Loy, to the masculinist model laid down by Futurism, the new wave of manifestos included cyberfeminist and trans- or post-humanist texts like Donna Haraway's *A Cyborg Manifesto* (1985/1991), Orlan's *Manifesto of Carnal Art* (1989) and VNS Matrix's *Cyberfeminist Manifesto for the 21ˢᵗ Century* (1991). These in turn anticipated more recent fourth-wave examples like *The Glitch Feminism Manifesto* (2012), *The Riot Code Grrrl Manifesto* (2015), *The Xenofeminist Manifesto* (2015) and the *Feminist Internet Manifesto* (2017). It would no doubt surprise Marinetti and the other Italian Futurists—or would it?—to learn that, a century later, they have been thrown "in the wastebasket like useless manuscripts" not by "younger and stronger men" but by a new generation of women critically engaged with technology and the future.

93. Bodies in protest

Manifestos can take many forms: letters, poems, posters, performances and so on. Rhetorical flourishes often mix with direct action. Manifestos can involve bodies, not only metaphorically but actually, physically, in performance or protest. As Sara Ahmed writes: "In the labor of making manifest we make a manifesto." Bodies have been used symbolically in protests for centuries: the start of the Arab Spring with the self-immolation of Tunisian street-vendor Mohamed Bouazizi in December 2010 is one recent example. But a similar case in New York in 2018—involving the death of civil rights lawyer and environmental advocate David Buckel—is notable for the way it brings together manifesto writing, direct action and the threat of catastrophic climate change. Just before dawn on April 14 Buckel doused himself in gasoline and lit himself on fire in Prospect Park, near his home in Brooklyn, dying of his injuries before responders arrived. Minutes earlier Buckel had sent an email to media outlets including *The New York Times* to explain his actions—a statement that reads like a manifesto in its elevated rhetorical style and passionate commitment to a cause. (There was also a paper note left at the scene.) "Pollution ravages our planet," the message begins. "Most humans on the planet now breathe air made unhealthy by fossil fuels, and many die early deaths as a result—my early death by fossil fuel reflects what we are doing to ourselves." Frustrated with the limitations of words and the kinds of small-scale individual action he was already taking, he resorted to a drastic symbolic act intended to encourage as many people as possible to hear his message and become engaged. We are seeing more and more of this in the twenty-first century: the manifesto as suicide note. In Buckel's case his premature death was to raise awareness for an urgent cause. In some very different cases discussed elsewhere in this book, however, there is a sort of death by narcissism — a violent act such as a mass shooting, driven by hatred and the desire to spread racist or misogynistic ideas, paired with a solipsistic screed. This is a worrying trend that brings together some of the most fundamental challenges we face: isolation, narcissism, lack of empathy, the blurring of fantasy and reality. In Buckel's case, however, the opposite was true: the dedicated activist felt powerless in the face of climate change, and his suicide was the ultimate gesture of empathy to the millions who will suffer and are already suffering as a result.

94. Manifestos of the Anthropocene

As we travel deeper into what an increasing number of researchers are calling the Anthropocene to describe the changed conditions we are living in—the epoch of the artificial—extreme climate change scenarios are now not only looming menacingly in our near future but can even be experienced in the present as a kind of "future shock." ("Future shock" is defined in the classic 1970 book by Alvin Toffler as "too much change in too short a period of time.") In another sense climate change may be added to the list of "shocks" (media, advertising, etc.) that characterize the traumatic experience of modernity itself—the shocks that overwhelm our comprehension of the world, confronting us with more information than we can process. Walter Benjamin wrote about the shocks of modernity in his essay "On Some Motifs in Baudelaire" (1939), where he also introduces the figure of the *flâneur* using the example of Edgar Allen Poe's short story, "The Man of the Crowd" (1840). Added to our shock is the sense that we must do something, anything, while at the same time we may feel both helpless to act and strangely at home in the "new normal." Born out of modernity, manifestos have always been both a reflection of and a shaping force on the future— and therefore they are essential to any attempt we make to deal with climate futures, whether psychologically or actually. Like their feminist peers, what might loosely be termed ecological manifestos have a long history: from hippie manifestos of the 1960s like *The Unanimous Declaration of Interdependence* (published in *Holocene Gazette and Country Traveller* in 1969), to Donna Haraway's *Companion Species Manifesto* (2003), "a political act of hope in a world on the edge of global war," to a new generation of digital age manifestos including Alex Williams and Nick Srnicek's *Manifesto for an Accelerationist Politics* (2013) and Daniel Rourke and Morehshin Allahyari's *The 3D Additivist*

Manifesto (2015), to similarly apocalyptic but more neo-Luddite "dark ecology" manifestos such as Dougald Hine and Paul Kingsnorth's *Uncivilisation: The Dark Mountain Manifesto* (2009), which declares that "There is a fall coming" and warns: "We do not believe that everything will be fine."

95. The uplifting conclusion

At the end of the 2010s it is hard to argue that everything will be fine. As some of the manifestos in the previous section make clear, technology is not the thing that is killing us so much as capitalism: our desire, addiction, distraction and consumption. The two things aren't easy to separate, of course, and technology isn't neutral—as Cameron Tonkinwise has stated, "Design is both the product of and the producer of modernism." So what can manifestos do? Well, as *The Communist Manifesto* continues to prove on Marx's two-hundredth birthday, manifestos make useful tools of theory and critique—often more useful, it has to be said, than sober and practical maps for the future. What else? Manifestos tend to appear at times of radical upheaval, claiming to offer answers or a path through the crisis. The more broken and ineffectual the normal channels seem, the more reassuring is the manifesto's confident tone, and the more people look for bold new disruptive alternatives. When civic systems and civil behavior fails, quasi-civic and "uncivil" forms of protest are needed to disrupt the status quo and overcome barriers to justice. Manifestos provide hope in an era of political hopelessness. They help us steady our gaze on the big picture, rather than being kept constantly distracted and disoriented by the daily news cycle. As I write this, debates are circling in the US about the loss of civility in public life, with some voices seeming to suggest that protest itself should be disallowed if it is deemed uncivil. The avant-garde manifesto is the *ur*-genre of incivility—to cause offense to the status quo is both its aim and its modus operandi. Revolution and disruption are uncivil. But what if no one is less civil than the commander in chief? How do we disrupt disruption? Should we, like Gilbert and George, remain "relaxed and friendly polite and in complete control"? Or, like the Accelerationists, do we take disruption as far as it can possibly go—in the hope of hastening revolutionary change? Whatever you do, dear reader, when you write a manifesto, be *brave*. Manifestos have no idols; there is no moderation. Any manifesto worth reading or writing must demand the impossible. Manifestos are safe spaces for audacity and ambition, even in this thin-skinned age. Nothing is too extreme, too overreaching, too far out or over the top. Paint in bold strokes. Don't let silly facts get in the way. This is naked polemic, not an address to the debating society. Your judge is not sitting on Twitter or even on the US Supreme Court—your only judge is history.

Bibliography

Preface

Douglas Coupland, *City of Glass* (Toronto: Douglas & McIntyre, 2000).

Luigi Russolo, "The Art of Noises" [1913], in *Futurist Manifestos*, ed. Umbro Apollonio (Boston: MFA, 2001), pp. 74-88.

Marinetti quoted in Luca Somigli, *Legitimizing the Artist: Manifesto Writing and European Modernism, 1885-1915* (Toronto: University of Toronto Press, 2003), p. 97.

Ioana Georgescu's Artist Page: http://www.ioanageorgescu.com

Chris Kraus, *I Love Dick* (Los Angeles: Semiotext(e), 1997), p. 29.

Wyndham Lewis, *The Letters of Wyndham Lewis*, ed. W. K. Rose (London: Methuen, 1963), p. 309.

Sara Ahmed, *Living a Feminist Life* (Durham: Duke University Press, 2017), p. 252.

Introduction

Tristan Tzara, "Dada Manifesto" [1918], in *Manifesto: A Century of Isms*, ed. Mary Ann Caws (Lincoln: University of Nebraska Press, 2001), p. 297.

Bruno Latour, "An Attempt at a 'Compositionist Manifesto,'" *New Literary History* 41 (2010): pp. 471-90, p. 473.

Marjorie Perloff, *The Futurist Moment: Avant-Garde, Avant Guerre, and the Language of Rupture* (Chicago and London: Chicago University Press, 2003), p. 82.

Ottessa Moshfegh, *My Year of Rest and Relaxation* (London and New York: Penguin, 2018).

Robert Lowell, "Memories of West Street and Lepke," in *Life Studies* (New York: Vintage, 1959).

Gay Liberation Front, "Manifesto" [1971], in Peter Stansill and David Zane Mairowitz (eds.), *BAMN (By Any Means Necessary): Outlaw Manifestos and Ephemera 1965-70* (New

York: Autonomedia, 1999), p. 200.

"Queers Read This" (1990): http://www.qrd.org/qrd/misc/text/queers.read.this

FM-2030 (Fereidoun M. Esfandiary), *UpWingers: A Futurist Manifesto* (New York: John Day, 1973).

Marshall McLuhan, *Counterblast* (Toronto: McClelland and Stewart, 1969), p. 53.

Joyce Carol Oates, "Notes on Failure," *The Hudson Review* 35.2 (1982): pp. 231-45, p. 232.

J. L. Austin, *How to Do Things with Words* (New York and Oxford: Oxford University Press, 1965).

Valerie Solanas, *SCUM Manifesto* [1967], ed. Avital Ronell (London and New York: Verso, 2004).

F. T. Marinetti, "The Founding and Manifesto of Futurism" [1909], in Apollonio, *Futurist Manifestos*, p. 22.

Tom Holland (@holland_tom) on Twitter (July 7, 2018).

Walter Gropius, "Bauhaus Manifesto and Program" (1919): http://mariabuszek.com/mariabuszek/kcai/ConstrBau/Readings/GropBau19.pdf

Libby Sellers, *Women Design* (London: Frances Lincoln, 2018).

Victor Khlebnikov and others, "The Trumpet of the Martians" [1916], in Caws, *Manifesto*, p. 238.

Marianne Moore, "The Hero," in *Complete Poems* (London and New York: Penguin, 1994), pp. 8-9.

"MJ's 'Manifesto,' Penned in 1979," CBS News (2013): https://www.cbsnews.com/news/mjs-manifesto-penned-in-1979/

Wyndham Lewis, *BLAST* 1 [1914] (Santa Barbara: Black Sparrow, 1981), p. 8.

Jon Ronson, *So You've Been Publicly Shamed* (London: Picador, 2015).

95 Theses on an Incendiary Form

1.

Caws, *Manifesto*, p. 297.

2.

Karl Marx and Friedrich Engels, *The Communist Manifesto* (London and New York: Penguin, 2002), p. 218.

3.

Apollonio, *Futurist Manifestos*, pp. 19-21.

4.

Umberto Boccioni, Carlo Carrà, Luigi Russolo, Giacomo Balla and Gino Severini, "Futurist Painting: Technical Manifesto" [1910], in Apollonio, *Futurist Manifestos*, p. 27.

5.

George Carlin interviewed by John Stewart (1997), YouTube: https://youtu.be/nCGGWeD_EJk

6.

Eric Hobsbawm, "A Century of Manifestos," in *Serpentine Gallery Manifesto Marathon*, ed. Nicola Lees (London: Koenig, 2009), p. 97.

7.

Peter Steiner, "On the internet, nobody knows you're a dog," *The New Yorker* (July 5, 1993).

8.

Wyndham Lewis, "The Vorticists" [1956], in *Creatures of Habit and Creatures of Change*, ed. Paul Edwards (Santa Rosa: Black Sparrow, 1989), p. 382.

9.

In W. H. Auden and Louis Kronenberger (eds.), *The Faber Book of Aphorisms* (London: Faber, 1974), p. 282.

Pierre Restany and Yves Klein, *Manifeste du Nouveau Réalisme*, 1960.

10.

Étienne Léro and others, *Légitime Défense Manifesto* [1932], in *Why Are We "Artists"? 100 World Art Manifestos*, ed. Jessica Lack (London and New York: Penguin, 2017), p. 22.

King Mob, "We Are Outlaws" [1968], in Stansill and Mairowitz, *BAMN*, p. 11.

Friedrich Nietzsche, *The Gay Science* [1887], trans. Josefine Nauckhoff (Cambridge and New York: Cambridge University Press, 2001), p. 230.

11.

Wyndham Lewis, *Blasting and Bombardiering* [1937] (London and New York: John Calder and Riverrun, 1982), p. 32.

12.

Authors Take Sides on the Spanish War [1937] (London: Cecil Woolf, 2001).

13.

James McNeill Whistler, *The Gentle Art of Making Enemies* [1890] (London: Heinemann, 1953).

14.

Oscar Wilde, *The Picture of Dorian Gray* (Peterborough, ON: Broadview, 2005), pp. 41-2.

Derek Jarman, *Modern Nature* (London: Vintage, 2018), p. 196.

15.

Walter Benjamin, *Illuminations*, trans. Harry Zohn (New York: Schocken, 2007), pp. 241-2.

16.

Boaventura de Sousa Santos, *Epistemologies of the South* (Boulder, CO: Paradigm, 2014), p. 3.

David Graeber, *Fragments of an Anarchist Anthropology* (Chicago: Prickly Paradigm Press, 2004).

Jean (Hans) Arp, "Infinite Millimeter Manifesto" [1938], in Caws, *Manifesto*, p. 293.

Friedrich Nietzsche, *Twilight of the Idols* [1889], in *The Portable Nietzsche*, ed. Walter Kaufman (New York: Viking, 1982), p. 556.

17.

Stanley Brouwn, "A Short Manifesto" [1964], in *100 Artists' Manifestos*, ed. Alex Danchev (London and New York: Penguin, 2011), p. 372.

Gilbert and George, "The Laws of Sculptors" [1969], in Danchev, *100 Manifestos*, p. 380.

18.

Adolf Hitler, *Mein Kampf* [1925], trans. Ralph Manheim (London: Pimlico, 1992).

Ted Kaczynski, *Industrial Society and Its Future* (Eugene, OR: Anti-Authoritarians Anonymous, 1995).

Anders Behring Breivik, *2083: A European Declaration of Independence* (2011): https://publicintelligence.net/anders-behring-breiviks-complete-manifesto-2083-a-european-declaration-of-independence/

André Breton, *Manifestoes of Surrealism*, trans. Richard Seaver and Helen R. Lane (Ann Arbor: University of Michigan Press, 1969).

19.

Donna Haraway, *Manifestly Haraway* (Minneapolis and London: University of Minnesota Press, 2016), p. 5.

20.

Jeffrey Goldberg, "A Senior White House Official Defines the Trump Doctrine: 'We're America, Bitch,'" *The Atlantic* (June 11, 2018).

21.

Valentine de Saint-Point, "Futurist Manifesto of Lust" [1913], in Caws, *Manifesto*, pp. 218-9.

Guillaume Apollinaire, "The Musician of Saint-Merri," *Zone: Selected Poems*, trans. Ron Padgett (New York: New York Review of Books, 2015), p. 143.

Claude Abastado quoted in Somigli, *Legitimizing the Artist*, p. 26.

22.

Tristan Tzara, "Note on Poetry" [1919], in Caws, *Manifesto*, p. 307.

F. T. Marinetti, "Manifesto of Futurist Playwrights: The Pleasures of Being Booed" [1910], in *Critical Writings*, ed. Günter Berghaus, trans. Doug Thompson (New York: Farrar, Straus and Giroux, 2006), p. 183.

Ian Bogost, "Who Needs Convertible Slippers?" *The Atlantic* (July 11, 2016).

23.

Lewis, *BLAST* 1, p. 7.

Fernando Pessoa, *Sensacionismo e Outros Ismos*, ed. Jerónimo Pizarro (Lisbon: Imprensa Nacional, 2009), p. 159.

24.

Lewis, *BLAST* 1, pp. 11-13.

F. T. Marinetti and others, "Futurist Synthesis of the War" [1914], in Caws, *Manifesto*, pp. 170-1.

Guillaume Apollinaire, "Cheval" [1913-16], in Caws, *Manifesto*, p. 126.

25.

George Maciunas, "Fluxus Manifesto" [1963], in Danchev, *100 Manifestos*, p. 363.

26.

André Breton, Diego Rivera and Leon Trotsky, "Manifesto: Towards a Free Revolutionary Art" [1938], in Danchev, *100 Manifestos*, p. 296.

27.

Antonin Artaud, *The Theater and Its Double*, trans. Mary Caroline Richards (New York: Grove Weidenfeld, 1958).

28.

Fernando Pessoa (as Álvaro de Campos), "ULTIMATUM" [1917], in *Selected Prose*, ed. and trans. Richard Zenith (New York: Grove, 2001), pp. 72-3.

Oscar Wilde, *The Artist as Critic: Critical Writings*, ed. Richard Ellmann (Chicago: University of Chicago Press, 1982).

Ian Parker, "Glenn Greenwald: The Bane of Their Resistance," *The New Yorker* (September 3, 2018).

29.

F. T. Marinetti, "Self-Portrait" [1929], in *Critical Writings*, p. 8.

30.

Black Panther Party, "The Ten-Point Program" (1966), Marxists Internet Archive: https://www.marxists.org/history/usa/ workers/black-panthers/1966/10/15.htm

Dieter Rams, "Ten Principles for Good Design": https://www. vitsoe.com/gb/about/good-design

Guy Debord, Attila Kotányi and Raoul Vaneigem, "Theses on the Paris Commune" [1962], in *Situationist International Anthology*, ed. and trans. Ken Knabb (Berkeley: Bureau of Public Secrets, 2006), pp. 827-35.

31.

Anthony Dunne and Fiona Raby, "Manifesto": http://www. dunneandraby.co.uk/content/projects/476/0

Wyndham Lewis, "Manifesto I," *BLAST* 1, pp. 11-28.

Guillaume Apollinaire, "L'Antitradition-futuriste" [1913], in Caws, *Manifesto*, p. 212.

32.

Maggie Nelson, *Bluets* (Seattle and New York: Wave, 2009).

Charles and Ray Eames, "Design Q&A" (1972): http://www. eamesoffice.com/the-work/design-q-a-text/

"Ghent Manifesto" (2018): https://www.ntgent.be/en/manifest

F. T. Marinetti, "Manifesto of Futurist Cuisine" [1930], in *Critical Writings*, pp. 394-9.

33.

David Foster Wallace, "Deciderization 2007: A Special Report," in *Both Flesh and Not: Essays* (New York: Back Bay Books, 2012), p. 301.

34.

Frank O'Hara, "Personism: A Manifesto" [1959], in Caws, *Manifesto*, p. 592.

Quoted in Stansill and Mairowitz, *BAMN*, p. 41.

35.

D. H. Lawrence, "Manifesto" [1916], in *Complete Poems*, 2 vols., eds. Vivian de Sola Pinto and Warren Roberts (London: Heinemann, 1972), p. 265.

W. H. Auden, "Spain" [1937], in *Poetry of the Thirties*, ed. Robin Skelton (London and New York: Penguin, 2000), p. 136.

36.

David Joselit, Joan Simon and Renata Saleci (eds.), *Jenny Holzer* (New York and London: Phaidon, 2010).

F. T. Marinetti, "The Necessity and Beauty of Violence" [1910], in *Critical Writings*, pp. 60-72.

Joanna Walsh, *Break.up* (Pasadena, CA: Semiotext(e), 2018), p. 260.

37.

F. T. Marinetti, "Lecture to the English on Futurism" [1910], in *Critical Writings*, p. 89.

Francis Picabia, "Dada Cannibalistic Manifesto" [1920], in Caws, *Manifesto*, p. 316.

38.

John Sinclair, "White Panther Manifesto" [1968], in Stansill and Mairowitz, *BAMN*, pp. 164-6.

Hate Socialist Collective, "Leave the Manifesto Alone: A Manifesto," *Poetry*, February 2009: https://www. poetryfoundation.org/poetrymagazine/articles/69203/leave-the-manifesto-alone-a-manifesto

The Angry Brigade, "Communiqué 1" [1970], in *The Angry Brigade: Documents and Chronology, 1967-1984* (London: Elephant Editions, 1985), p. 10.

Greil Marcus, *Lipstick Traces: A Secret History of the Twentieth Century* (London: Faber, 2001).

Ben Beaumont-Thomas, "Stormzy asks 'Theresa May, where's the money for Grenfell?' at Brit Awards," *The Guardian* (February 21, 2018).

R. B. Kitaj, "First Diasporist Manifesto" [1989], in Danchev, *100 Manifestos*, p. 406.

39.

Avital Ronell, "The Deviant Payback: The Aims of Valerie Solanas," in Solanas, *SCUM*, p. 3.

40.

Jarman, *Modern Nature*, p. 126.

Ezra Pound, "The New Sculpture," *The Egoist*, 1.4 (16 February 1914), pp. 67-8.

Lewis, *Blasting*, p. 36.

41.

Ahmed, *Living a Feminist Life*, p. 252.

Solanas, *SCUM*, p. 76.

Jessa Crispin, *Why I Am Not a Feminist: A Feminist Manifesto* (Brooklyn: Melville House, 2018), p. xii.

Marx and Engels, *The Communist Manifesto*, p. 237.

Oona A. Hathaway, William Holste, Scott J. Shapiro, Jacqueline Van De Velde and Lisa Wang, *War Manifestos Database* (2017): http://documents.law.yale.edu/manifestos

42.

Daniel Rourke in an email, October 26, 2015.

43.

John Perry Barlow, "A Declaration of the Independence of Cyberspace" (1996), Electronic Frontier Foundation: https://www.eff.org/cyberspace-independence

44.

Marina Abramović, "An Artist's Life Manifesto," in Lees, *Manifesto Marathon*, pp. 36-7.

VNS Matrix, "Cyberfeminist Manifesto for the 21st Century" [1991], in *Manifestos for the Internet Age* (Greyscale Press, 2015), p. 37.

Stansill and Mairowitz, *BAMN*, p. 165.

Janet Lyon, *Manifestoes: Provocations of the Modern* (Ithaca and London: Cornell University Press, 1999), pp. 34 and 105.

Rebecca Solnit, *Wanderlust: A History of Walking* (London and New York: Penguin, 2001).

Ahmed, *Living a Feminist Life*, p. 255.

Chimamanda Ngozi Adichie, *Dear Ijeawele, or, A Feminist Manifesto in Fifteen Suggestions* (New York: Knopf, 2017).

Lack, *100 World Art*, p. 21.

45.

Guillaume Apollinaire, "The New Spirit and the Poets" [1918], in *Art in Theory: 1900-1990*, eds. Charles Harrison and Paul Wood (Oxford and Malden, MA: Blackwood, 2001), p. 226.

46.

David Burliuk, Alexander Kruchenykh, Vladimir Mayakovsky and Victor Khlebnikov, "Slap in the Face of Public Taste" [1912], in Anna Lawton and Herbert Eagle (eds.), *Russian Futurism Through Its Manifestoes, 1912-1928* (Ithaca and London: Cornell University Press, 1988), p. 51.

Caws, *Manifesto*, p. 188.

47.

David Hockney, "Manifesto for Smoking," in Lees, *Manifesto Marathon*, pp. 102-3.

Derek Jarman, "Manifesto" [1964], in Danchev, *100 Manifestos*, p. 375.

Kirill Medvedev, *It's No Good*, ed. and trans. Keith Gessen (New York: n+1, 2012), p. 147.

48.

Caws, *Manifesto*, p. 300.

F. S. Flint, "Imagisme" [1913], in Caws, *Manifesto*, p. 352.

Peyami Safa, "D Group Manifesto" [1933], in Lack, *100 World Art*, p. 27.

Timothy Morton, *Being Ecological* (New York and London: Pelican, 2018), p. 3.

Karl Marx, *The Eighteenth Brumaire of Louis Bonaparte* (1852), Marxists Internet Archive: https://www.marxists.org/archive/marx/works/download/pdf/18th-Brumaire.pdf

49.

Martin Puchner, "Manifesto = Theatre," in Lees, *Manifesto Marathon*, p. 18.

Joichi Ito, "Resisting Reduction: A Manifesto" (2017), *Journal of Design and Science*: https://jods.mitpress.mit.edu/pub/resisting-reduction

Radical Change in Culture, "Manifesto," *Variant* 37 (Spring / Summer 2010): http://www.variant.org.uk/pdfs/issue37_38/V37edit_manif.pdf

Chris Packham, "A People's Manifesto for Wildlife" (2018): http://www.chrispackham.co.uk/a-peoples-manifesto-for-wildlife

Rosa Menkman, "Glitch Studies Manifesto" (2010): http://rosa-menkman.blogspot.com/2010/02/glitch-studies-manifesto.html

Robert Pepperell, "The Posthuman Manifesto" (2005): https://intertheory.org/pepperell.htm

Cary Nelson, *Manifesto of a Tenured Radical* (New York and London: New York University Press, 1997).

Garnet Hertz, *Disobedient Electronics: Protest* (2016): http://www.disobedientelectronics.com

Trebor Scholz and Nathan Schneider (eds.), *Ours to Hack and Own* (New York: OR Books, 2017), p. 10.

50.

Virginia Woolf, *A Writer's Diary*, ed. Leonard Woolf (San Diego: Harvest, 1982), p. 10.

51.

Virginia Woolf, *A Room of One's Own and Three Guineas* (New York and Oxford: Oxford University Press, 2000), pp. 202, 155, 168, 229.

52.

Ibid., pp. 252 and 366.

53.

F. T. Marinetti, Emilio Settimelli and Bruno Corra, "The Futurist Synthetic Theater" [1915], in Apollonio, *Futurist Manifestos*, p. 196.

Solanas, *SCUM*, p. 64.

Stanley Kubrick, dir., *Full Metal Jacket* (Warner Bros. Pictures, 1987).

54.

Martin Puchner, "Screeching Voices: Avant-Garde Manifestos in the Cabaret," in *European Avant-Garde: New Perspectives*, ed. Dietrich Scheunemann (Amsterdam: Rodopi, 2000), p. 114.

55.

Caws, *Manifesto*, p. 300.

Lewis, *Creatures of Habit*, p. 382.

Apollonio, *Futurist Manifestos*, p. 23.

56.

Margaret Atwood, *Second Words: Selected Critical Prose* (Toronto: Anansi, 1982), p. 413.

Reading of the Front de Libération du Québec (FLQ)

Manifesto on Radio-Canada (1970), YouTube: https://youtu. be/0SBW5pog8bg

Elliot Rodger, "Manifesto," *The New York Times* (May 25, 2014).

Cory Doctorow, *Down and Out in the Magic Kingdom* (New York: Tor, 2003).

Bob Woodward, *Fear: Trump in the White House* (New York: Simon & Schuster, 2018).

57.

Valentine de Saint-Point, "Manifesto of Futurist Woman" [1912], in Caws, *Manifesto*, p. 215.

Solanas, *SCUM*, p. 35.

Crispin, *Why I Am Not a Feminist*, p. xi.

Ahmed, *Living a Feminist Life*, p. 253.

Dylann Roof, "Manifesto," *The New York Times* (December 13, 2016).

58.

Caws, *Manifesto*, p. 307.

Bruno Latour, "A Cautious Prometheus? A Few Steps Toward a Philosophy of Design (with Special Attention to Peter Sloterdijk)" (2008): http://www.bruno-latour.fr/node/69

David Shrigley, *Weak Messages Create Bad Situations: A Manifesto* (Edinburgh: Canongate, 2014).

59.

Malcolm Bradbury and James McFarlane (eds.), *Modernism: 1890-1930* (New York and London: Penguin, 1976), p. 202.

Vladimir Mayakovsky, "We, Too, Want Meat!" [1914], in Caws, *Manifesto*, p. 232.

Margaret Atwood, "Am I a Bad Feminist?" *The Globe and Mail* (January 13, 2018).

60.

Caws, *Manifesto*, p. 297.

Lauren Shumway, "The Intelligibility of the Avant-Garde Manifesto," *French Literature Series* 7 (1980), p. 57.

James Longenbach, *Stone Cottage: Pound, Yeats, and Modernism* (New York and Oxford: Oxford University Press, 1991).

Lyon, *Manifestoes*, p. 131.

Theodor Adorno, "The Essay as Form," *New German Critique* 32 (1984), p. 157.

Caws, *Manifesto*, p. 302.

Tristan Tzara and others, "Dada Excites Everything" [1921], in Caws, *Manifesto*, p. 290.

61.

Perry Anderson, *The Origins of Postmodernity* (London and New York: Verso, 1998), p. 93.

62.

David Gascoyne, *Selected Prose 1934-1996*, ed. Roger Scott (London: Enitharmon, 1998), p. 457.

Mina Loy, *The Lost Lunar Baedeker*, ed. Roger Conover (Manchester: Carcanet, 1997).

Melissa Gronlund, "The Manifesto: What's in it for Us?" in Lees, *Manifesto Marathon*, pp. 12-16.

63.

Georges Perec, *Species of Spaces and Other Pieces*, ed. and trans. John Sturrock (London and New York: Penguin, 1999), p. 185.

William Morris, *News from Nowhere* (New York and Oxford: Oxford University Press, 2009).

64.

David Edgerton, *The Shock of the Old: Technology and Global History Since 1900* (New York and Oxford: Oxford University

Press, 2007).

Oscar Wilde, "The Soul of Man Under Socialism" [1891], in *Critical Writings*, p. 269.

Fredric Jameson, *Postmodernism, or, The Cultural Logic of Late Capitalism* (Durham, NC: Duke University Press, 1991).

Franco "Bifo" Berardi, *After the Future* (Chico, CA: AK Press, 2011).

James Bridle, *New Dark Age* (London and Brooklyn: Verso, 2018), p. 252.

65.

The Seasteading Institute, "The Eight Great Moral Imperatives": https://www.seasteading.org/videos/the-eight-great-moral-imperatives/

Wayne Gramlich, "Seasteading: Homesteading on the High Seas" (1998): http://gramlich.net/projects/oceania/seastead1.html

Peter Thiel, "The Education of a Libertarian" (2009): https://www.cato-unbound.org/2009/04/13/peter-thiel/education-libertarian

66.

Danchev, *100 Manifestos*, p. 374.

Jarman, *Modern Nature*, p. 179.

Lees, *Manifesto Marathon*, p. 7.

Bruce Sterling, "The Dead Media Manifesto" (1998): http://www.alamut.com/subj/artiface/deadMedia/dM_Manifesto.html

68.

Caws, *Manifesto*, xxii.

Nicholas Mirzoeff, *How to See the World* (London and New York: Pelican, 2015), p. 5.

70.

Nick Montfort, *The Future* (Cambridge, MA and London: MIT Press, 2017), p. xii.

Scott Smith, "Beware of Flat-Pack Futures" (2013): https://vimeo.com/66314529

71.

Jorge Carrión, "Against Amazon: Seven Arguments, One Manifesto" (2017): https://lithub.com/against-amazon-seven-arguments-one-manifesto/

Garnet Hertz, "The Maker's Bill of Rights" (2018): https://monoskop.org/images/e/e7/Hertz_Garnet_2018_The_Makers_Bill_of_Rights.pdf

72.

Laboria Cuboniks, "Xenofeminism: A Politics for Alienation" (2015): http://www.laboriacuboniks.net

"Patricia Reed on Xenofeminism," Politics Theory Other podcast #3 (April 2018): https://soundcloud.com/poltheoryother/3-patricia-reed-on-xenofeminism

Frank Kolkman, OpenSurgery (2015): http://www.opensurgery.net

73.

Walter Benjamin, "Theses on the Philosophy of History," in *Illuminations*, p. 257.

Mina Loy, "Feminist Manifesto" [1914], in *Lost Lunar Baedeker*, p. 155.

Lewis, *BLAST* 1, p. 151.

74.

Eugene Jolas and others, "The Revolution of the Word" [1929], in Caws, *Manifesto*, p. 531.

Oswald de Andrade, "Cannibalist Manifesto" [1928], in Danchev,

100 Manifestos, pp. 263-6.

Uche Okeke, "Natural Synthesis" [1960], in Lack, *100 World Art*, p. 62.

Lucio Fontana, "White Manifesto" [1946], in Danchev, *100 Manifestos*, pp. 305-11.

75.

Dave Beech, Andy Hewitt and Mel Jordan (The Freee Art Collective), "The New Futurist Manifesto," *Third Text* 23.5 (2009): 587-92: p. 589.

76.

Laura Beiles, "Words in Freedom: Futurism at 100" (2009), MoMA. org: https://www.moma.org/interactives/exhibitions/2009/futurism/

Edward Denison, Guang Yu Ren and Niagzy Gebremedhin (eds.), *Asmara: Africa's Secret Modernist City* (London and New York: Merrell, 2006).

Agnès Varda, "What To Do? How To Do It? (A Potato Story)," in Lees, *Manifesto Marathon*, p. 207.

77.

F. T. Marinetti, "Against Traditionalist Venice," in *Critical Writings*, p. 166.

Julian Hanna and Yanina Spizzirri, "Now Is the Time: A Manifesto for Minor Literature[s]," *minor literature[s]* (October 5, 2016): https://minorliteratures.com/2016/10/05/now-is-the-time-a-manifesto-for-minor-literatures-julian-hanna-and-yanina-spizzirri/

Julian Hanna and Yanina Spizzirri, "BLAST FASCISM," *minor literature[s]* (September 15, 2017): https://minorliteratures.com/2017/09/15/blast-fascism-the-minor-literatures-anti-fascist-manifesto/

78.

Grimes (Claire Boucher), "The Faé List" (September 26, 2017), Tumblr: http://grimes-claireboucher.tumblr.com/

William Gibson, *Burning Chrome* (New York: Ace Books, 1987), p. 186.

79.

Quinn Norton, "*The New York Times* Fired My Doppelgänger," *The Atlantic* (February 27, 2018).

80.

Jaron Lanier, *Ten Arguments for Deleting Your Social Media Accounts Right Now* (New York: Henry Holt, 2018), p. 67.

81.

Lewis, *BLAST* 1, p. 8.

Benjamin Noys, *Malign Velocities: Accelerationism and Capitalism* (Alresford, Hants: Zero Books, 2014).

Attaque, "Arson at La Casemate Fablab, Center for Scientific, Technical, and Industrial Culture of Grenoble" (December 6, 2017), Earth First! Journal: https://earthfirstjournal.org/newswire/2017/12/06/france-arson-at-la-casemate-fablab-center-for-scientific-technical-and-industrial-culture-of-grenoble/

Slow Food, "Slow Food Manifesto" (1989): https://www.slowfood.com/about-us/key-documents/

Slow Media, "The Slow Media Manifesto" (2010): http://en.slow-media.net/manifesto

Vincenzo Di Nicola, "Slow Thought: A Manifesto," *Aeon* (February 27, 2018): https://aeon.co/essays/take-your-time-the-seven-pillars-of-a-slow-thought-manifesto

82.

McKenzie Wark, *A Hacker Manifesto* (Cambridge, MA and

London: Harvard University Press, 2004), section 004.

European Pirate Party, "PP-EU Manifesto" (2013): http://wiki. piratpartiet.no/PP-EU_Manifesto

James Joyce, *Finnegans Wake* [1939] (New York and London: Penguin, 2000).

Bre Pettis and Kio Stark, "The Cult of Done Manifesto" (2009), Medium: https://medium.com/@bre/the-cult-of-done-manifesto-724ca1c2ff13

V2_, "Manifesto for the Unstable Media" (1987): http://v2.nl/ events/manifest

83.

Edward Snowden, "A Manifesto for the Truth" [2013], in *Manifestos for the Internet Age*, pp. 145-6.

Aaron Swartz, "Guerilla Open Access Manifesto" [2008], in Ibid., pp. 90-92.

Cody Wilson at the Design & Violence Debate (2014), YouTube: https://youtu.be/sKB471lRfZg

Andy Greenberg, "A Landmark Legal Shift Opens Pandora's Box for DIY Guns," *Wired* (July 10, 2018): https://www.wired. com/story/a-landmark-legal-shift-opens-pandoras-box-for-diy-guns/

84.

Toby Litt, "Johnny Ruin by Dan Dalton review — for the love of a Manic Pixie Dream Girl," *The Guardian* (April 12, 2018).

Kenneth Goldsmith, *Wasting Time on the Internet* (New York: HarperCollins, 2016).

85.

Ganzeer, "Manifesto Everything" (2018): http://www.ganzeer. com/post/172142377024/theres-too-much-stuff-pointless-stuff

Amber Johnson, "Why You Should Write a Manifesto for

Everything You Do" (2017), *Science of Story*: https://scienceofstory.org/writing-a-manifesto-for-everything-you-do/

86.

Gwyneth Paltrow, "What's Goop?" Goop: https://goop.com/whats-goop/

87.

Blaise Cendrars, "The ABCs of Cinema" [1917-21], in Caws, *Manifesto*, p. 155.

Solanas, *SCUM*, p. 69.

Martine Syms, "The Mundane Afrofuturist Manifesto," *Rhizome* (December 17, 2013): http://rhizome.org/editorial/2013/dec/17/mundane-afrofuturist-manifesto/

Editorial staff of *The Eagle Eye*, "Our Manifesto to Fix America's Gun Laws," *The Guardian* (March 23, 2018).

Caws, *Manifesto*, p. 189.

Ibid., p. 231.

88.

Anna Khachiyan, "Art Won't Save Us" (2018), Open Space: https://openspace.sfmoma.org/2018/03/art-wont-save-us/

Angela Nagle, *Kill All Normies: Online Culture Wars From 4Chan and Tumblr To Trump and The Alt-Right* (Alresford, Hants: Zero Books, 2017).

89.

We Are Not Surprised, "Original Letter" (2017): http://www.not-surprised.org/original-letter/

Jenny Holzer, *Inflammatory Essays* (1979-82), Tate: https://www.tate.org.uk/art/artworks/holzer-inflammatory-essays-65434

Jenny Holzer, "Anti-Gun Truck" (2018): http://projects.jennyholzer.com/anti-gun-truck

90.

We Are Not Surprised, "Second Letter" (2018): http://www.not-surprised.org/home/

Roberta Smith, "In a Mattress, a Lever for Art and Political Protest," *The New York Times* (September 21, 2014).

Sarah Chiche, Catherine Millet, Catherine Robbe-Grillet, Peggy Sastre and Abnousse Shalmani, "Anti-#MeToo Manifesto" (2018), *Le Monde* / Worldcrunch: https://www.worldcrunch.com/opinion-analysis/full-translation-of-french-anti-metoo-manifesto-signed-by-catherine-deneuve#

91.

Lyon, *Manifestoes*, pp. 168-202.

Kathleen Hanna, "Riot Grrrl Manifesto" (1991), History is a Weapon: https://www.historyisaweapon.com/defcon1/riotgrrrlmanifesto.html

Zoe Leonard, "I want a president" (1992): https://iwantapresident.wordpress.com/i-want-a-president-zoe-leonard-1992/

92.

Monty Cantsin, "Neoism Manifesto" (1979), Monoskop: https://monoskop.org/Neoism

Orlan, "Manifesto of Carnal Art" (1989): http://www.orlan.eu/texts/

Legacy Russell, "Digital Dualism and the Glitch Feminism Manifesto," *The Society Pages* (December 10, 2012): https://thesocietypages.org/cyborgology/2012/12/10/digital-dualism-and-the-glitch-feminism-manifesto/

Lindsey Bieda, "Riot Code Grrrl Manifesto" (2015): https://rarlindseysmash.com/posts/riot-code-grrrl-manifesto

Feminist Internet, "The Feminist Internet Manifesto" (2017): https://www.feministinternet.com/manifesto

93.

Ahmed, *Living a Feminist Life*, p. 252.

Annie Correal, "What Drove a Man to Set Himself on Fire in Brooklyn?" *The New York Times* (May 28, 2018).

94.

"Anthropocene," Monoskop: https://monoskop.org/Anthropocene

Alvin Toffler, *Future Shock* (New York: Bantam Books, 1971), p. 2.

Jeffrey Ball, "With Climate Change No Longer in the Future, Adaptation Speeds Up," *The New York Times* (September 21, 2018).

Benjamin, *Illuminations*, pp. 155-200.

Stansill and Mairowitz, *BAMN*, p. 176.

Haraway, *Manifestly Haraway*, p. 95.

Alex Williams and Nick Srnicek, "Manifesto for an Accelerationist Politics," *Critical Legal Thinking* (May 14, 2013): http://criticallegalthinking.com/2013/05/14/accelerate-manifesto-for-an-accelerationist-politics/

Daniel Rourke and Morehshin Allahyari, "The 3D Additivist Manifesto" (2015): https://additivism.org/manifesto

Dougald Hine and Paul Kingsnorth, "Uncivilisation: The Dark Mountain Manifesto" (2009): https://dark-mountain.net/about/manifesto/

95.

Cameron Tonkinwise, "Design for Transitions—From and To What?" (2015), Critical Design / Critical Futures: http://www.cd-cf.org/articles/design-for-transitions-from-and-to-what/

Acknowledgments

I should start by thanking Vassiliki Kolocotroni (the manifesto queen), and the dedicated scholars who have helped write the history of this strange little genre: Mary Ann Caws, Marjorie Perloff, Janet Lyon, Martin Puchner, Günter Berghaus, Luca Somigli, Laura Winkiel and many others. I also want to thank the editors who've read my thoughts in various forms along the way: Andrew Gallix, Tomoé Hill, Christopher Schaberg, Tristan Foster, Joanna Walsh, Russell Bennetts, Yanina Spizzirri, Fernando Sdrigotti, Morehshin Allahyari, Daniel Rourke, Adrian Paterson, Anne Karhio, Álvaro Seiça, Ana Luísa Valdeira, Madalena Palmeirim, and (always) others. I want to thank Madeira Interactive Technologies Institute for giving me a home, and my friend and colleague James Auger for putting up with my deviant obsessions. Finally I want to thank Eric Craven for helping to bring the manifesto into everyday life, all the friends who have sent me manifestos over the years, and of course my family—to whom I dedicate this book.

Some of the material in this book appeared in different form in *3:AM*, *Minor Literature[s]*, *Hyperrhiz*, *E-rea*, *Cine Qua Non* and *Berfrois*. Also included here in slightly different form is the essay "Manifestos: A Manifesto," © 2014 by Julian Hanna, as first published on TheAtlantic.com

CULTURE, SOCIETY & POLITICS

Contemporary culture has eliminated the concept and public figure of the intellectual. A cretinous anti-intellectualism presides, cheer-led by hacks in the pay of multinational corporations who reassure their bored readers that there is no need to rouse themselves from their stupor. Zer0 Books knows that another kind of discourse – intellectual without being academic, popular without being populist – is not only possible: it is already flourishing. Zer0 is convinced that in the unthinking, blandly consensual culture in which we live, critical and engaged theoretical reflection is more important than ever before. If you have enjoyed this book, why not tell other readers by posting a review on your preferred book site.

Recent bestsellers from Zero Books are:

In the Dust of This Planet
Horror of Philosophy vol. 1
Eugene Thacker
In the first of a series of three books on the Horror of Philosophy,
In the Dust of This Planet offers the genre of horror as a way of
thinking about the unthinkable.
Paperback: 978-1-84694-676-9 ebook: 978-1-78099-010-1

Capitalist Realism
Is there No Alternative?
Mark Fisher
An analysis of the ways in which capitalism has presented itself
as the only realistic political-economic system.
Paperback: 978-1-84694-317-1 ebook: 978-1-78099-734-6

Rebel Rebel
Chris O'Leary
David Bowie: every single song. Everything you want to know,
everything you didn't know.
Paperback: 978-1-78099-244-0 ebook: 978-1-78099-713-1

Cartographies of the Absolute
Alberto Toscano, Jeff Kinkle
An aesthetics of the economy for the twenty-first century.
Paperback: 978-1-78099-275-4 ebook: 978-1-78279-973-3

Poor but Sexy
Culture Clashes in Europe East and West
Agata Pyzik
How the East stayed East and the West stayed West.
Paperback: 978-1-78099-394-2 ebook: 978-1-78099-395-9

Malign Velocities

Accelerationism and Capitalism

Benjamin Noys

Long listed for the Bread and Roses Prize 2015, *Malign Velocities* argues against the need for speed, tracking acceleration as the symptom of the ongoing crises of capitalism.

Paperback: 978-1-78279-300-7 ebook: 978-1-78279-299-4

Meat Market

Female Flesh under Capitalism

Laurie Penny

A feminist dissection of women's bodies as the fleshy fulcrum of capitalist cannibalism, whereby women are both consumers and consumed.

Paperback: 978-1-84694-521-2 ebook: 978-1-84694-782-7

Poor but Sexy

Culture Clashes in Europe East and West

Agata Pyzik

How the East stayed East and the West stayed West.

Paperback: 978-1-78099-394-2 ebook: 978-1-78099-395-9

Romeo and Juliet in Palestine

Teaching Under Occupation

Tom Sperlinger

Life in the West Bank, the nature of pedagogy and the role of a university under occupation.

Paperback: 978-1-78279-637-4 ebook: 978-1-78279-636-7

Sweetening the Pill
or How We Got Hooked on Hormonal Birth Control
Holly Grigg-Spall
Has contraception liberated or oppressed women? *Sweetening
the Pill* breaks the silence on the dark side of hormonal
contraception.
Paperback: 978-1-78099-607-3 ebook: 978-1-78099-608-0

Why Are We The Good Guys?
Reclaiming your Mind from the Delusions of Propaganda
David Cromwell
A provocative challenge to the standard ideology that Western
power is a benevolent force in the world.
Paperback: 978-1-78099-365-2 ebook: 978-1-78099-366-9

Readers of ebooks can buy or view any of these bestsellers by
clicking on the live link in the title. Most titles are published
in paperback and as an ebook. Paperbacks are available in
traditional bookshops. Both print and ebook formats are available
online.
Find more titles and sign up to our readers' newsletter
at http://www.johnhuntpublishing.com/culture-and-politics
Follow us on Facebook
at https://www.facebook.com/ZeroBooks
and Twitter at https://twitter.com/Zer0Books